Inside Belsen

Inside Belsen

HANNA LÉVY-HASS

Translated from the German by
RONALD TAYLOR

WITH AN INTRODUCTION BY
JANE CAPLAN

THE HARVESTER PRESS · SUSSEX
BARNES & NOBLE BOOKS · NEW JERSEY

First published in Great Britain in 1982 by
THE HARVESTER PRESS LIMITED
Publisher: John Spiers
16 Ship Street, Brighton, Sussex
and in the USA by
BARNES & NOBLE BOOKS
81 Adams Drive, Totowa, New Jersey, 07512

© 1979, Rotbuch Verlag, Berlin

© This translation, The Harvester Press Ltd., 1982

Introduction © Jane Caplan, 1982

First published as *Vielleicht war das alles erst der Anfang*
by Rotbuch Verlag GmbH, 1979

British Library Cataloguing in Publication Data

Lévy-Haas, Hanna
   Inside Belsen.
   1. Belsen (Concentration camp)
   I. Title   II. Vielleicht war das alles erst der
   Anfang. *English*
   365'.34'0924   D805.G3

   ISBN 0-7108-0355-9
   Barnes & Noble Books
   ISBN 0-389-20301-7

Typeset in 11 on 13 Bembo by Inforum Ltd, Portsmouth
Printed in Great Britain by
Mansell Limited, Witham, Essex

CONTENTS

INTRODUCTION

Hanna Lévy-Hass was Jugoslav by birth, the daughter of impoverished middle-class Jews living in Sarajevo. She trained as a teacher in the 1930s, and was working at a school in Montenegro in 1941 when the fascist invasion and dismemberment of Jugoslavia took place. 'Like everyone else', she says, she was active in the resistance after 1941, not only as a Jugoslav, but as a communist sympathiser. In 1943, following the capitulation of Italy, the Germans took direct control of the Italian zones in Jugoslavia, including Montenegro. Lévy-Hass faced a choice between awaiting probable deportation or joining the partisans in the mountains. In practice it was likely to have been only a choice between two different deaths, but for Lévy-Hass it was also an impossible choice. Although she wanted to go into the mountains, she was dissuaded by the knowledge that fellow Jews would have been shot in reprisal for her action. So she stayed, and was rounded up by the Gestapo. In the summer of 1944 she was deported to Bergen-Belsen.

If Auschwitz represents the ultimate achievement in mechanised genocide, Belsen, at another extreme, was for the months before its liberation in April 1945 the apotheosis of mass murder by systematic neglect. Set up in 1941, Belsen had first been a Russian prisoner-of-war camp. By the time Lévy-Haas was brought there, it had been taken over by the SS and turned into a complex concentration camp for various categories of Jews (see chapter 5). In its final catastrophic phase, from the winter of 1944, it was made into a literal dumping-ground for thousands of prisoners evacuated from other camps, including Auschwitz, as the Allied armies closed in on Germany. No effort was made by the

Belsen administration to provide for these people.

As tens of thousands of new inmates were dumped into the camp – in the single week of April 3–14, 1945, the number was 28,000 – the food supply was shut off, roll calls were stopped, and the starving inmates were left to their own devices. Typhus and diarrhea raged unchecked, corpses rotted in barracks and on dung heaps. Rats attacked living inmates, and the dead ones were eaten by starving prisoners. (Hilberg, p. 633)

Hanna Lévy-Hass lived in this and grappled with it in words which she wrote down at the time.

Terence des Pres, writing about the memoirs of death camp survivors, draws attention to the moral heroism of those authors:

Ordinary people, in no way different from ourselves, go through infernal agony; they keep moral sense and memory intact; and afterwards, they take upon themselves the pain of living through it again, in order to fix its detail and make it known. (des Pres, p. 50)

It doesn't diminish the pain of recollection to point out that a diary, as well as being rarer than memoirs, has a compulsion that no act of recall possesses. The fact that we, now, can read what she, then, wrote doesn't so much telescope time as release it in waves of agitation. Any diary to some extent mobilises our sense of time and place; but how many so violently convulse, by virtue of their content, the subtle oscillations between writer and reader, between then and now? In September 1944 Lévy-Hass writes:

Even if I wrote and wrote, page after page, I could never describe all the aspects of our wretchedness, never convey all the cruel details of our lives . . . It would be a waste of effort to try to describe it all. It lies far beyond my competence.

But the incompetence is not in her writing, but in our willingness as readers to understand a situation which we cannot imagine and which many of us would perhaps prefer really not to know. Belsen was a place where some human beings, the German authorities and guards, decided to put others before they died into a situation in which they could not be human, in which they continually betrayed their humanity and behaved like animals; not once, or for just a short time, but for months on end.

Belsen was not the only place where this decision was put into practice. There are many testimonies to its operation and to the act of survival. There are in addition a number of more distanced social and psychological analyses of the mechanisms of domination and endurance, some of them written by survivors, which systematically review testimony and interpret it. Although one may say that the basic context — the organisation of sustained mass killing, by various means — was universal in the camps, the testimony cannot be reduced to a single meaning, except perhaps that of bearing witness; in other ways, it is too diverse. The effort of interpretation is one which the reader must make for herself or himself. What distinguishes Hanna Lévy-Hass's diary is its explicitly political perspective. The obligation it then imposes on readers is not merely to feel compassion or anger or horror, but to consider precisely the questions Lévy-Hass asks from the cruel privilege of her experience.

The memories of many survivors testify to the profound

conviction in the death camps and the concentration camps that after such horrors the new world *must* be entirely, almost inconceivably different, utterly transformed by the unprecedented suffering and knowledge of the victims. Lévy-Hass reveals this in her diary when she writes, for example, of her impatience for the advent of the new age, or of the suffocating happiness she imagines herself feeling after the liberation of her country. For her, however, this shared conviction that the promise of the future must balance the degradation of the present is sharpened by her political belief in reason as the principle of social being. But this belief was falsified by the daily evidence that the only social experience for the prisoners in Belsen was a negative one, a common deprivation of the possibility of collective human behaviour. This, it seems to me, is why she writes with such anger and despair about the individual iniquity that surrounds her: the grasping for straws of privilege and status, the absolute incapacity of most of her fellow prisoners to find a morality appropriate to their circumstances, the utter collapse of solidarity and moral choice into an abyss of villainous individualism. Thus do men systematically steal food, exploit accidents of privilege, live better than others, while simply denying that 'this life of plenty that they enjoy does no harm to the other prisoners . . . They make out that their well-being has in no way been bought at the price of the misery of the non-privileged, the rest of the starving inmates of the camp. Nothing of the kind, they say, it's just their good fortune.' Lévy-Hass goes on,

People like this of course will give a quite different account of the camp, of the Germans and of everything that has gone on. Some will even take pleasant memories with them, memories of an enjoyable time, of the 'kindness' of the Germans.

There are, then, more ways than one to survive, and not all of them are heroic. The heroism of moral intactness is not the automatic gift of circumstance, but has to be struggled for in drastic conditions. That a community of this kind could, nevertheless, be built on occasion is illustrated by the behaviour of the women in the camp, and in particular by one episode recorded by Lévy-Hass. She thought that the men adapted less to deprivation and were physically and morally weaker than the women. But the women could sometimes 'steel themselves to find ways of remedying the situation and show real courage, even prepared, if necessary, to make sacrifices'. This, she says, was mainly for the sake of the children; but the episode she recounts, in which the women of her hut collectively took over the distribution of food and succesfully resisted the Jewish overseer's attempts to restore his system of corruption and favouritism, had a wider resonance for her. The defeat of this secondary tyranny and injustice strengthened her confidence and restored her sense of being able to learn and to act; to choose the integrity of social solidarity over the depravity of selfishness.

There is a link between this episode, and her conversations with a Jugoslav professor, recorded at some length in the final phase of the camp. The two of them discussed as marxists the *reasons* for most prisoners' despicable behaviour. The professor argues that morality 'does not apply in concentration camps', that survival is all, and that if one wants to help build the new world then one must simply survive by whatever means. Lévy-Hass remains unconvinced, even though the professor dresses his argument in a purportedly marxist proposition about the relation of mind and matter. In the extremity of Belsen's last weeks, she rejects his contention that mind 'is merely the sublimation of matter', that 'consequently it is natural and inevitable that matter will reject mind when mind is irrelevant and has become an anomaly'. She sees through this to reverse the proposition and its consequence of ruthless self-preservation. If the survival of humanity and morality are premised on one's own physical survival, then an insoluble paradox arises: the betrayal of humanity and morality in order to preserve them. But Lévy-Hass proposes a different relation. The individual is not alone the carrier of those values. If she or he dies, the values are not thereby extinguished. Rather, one extinguishes them in choosing to survive at whatever cost. When she ends by asking 'But is human life so precious that we can permit all these atrocities in order to preserve it?', we already know the answer.

In fact, Hanna Lévy-Hass did survive. In April 1945, as the war was being fought to a conclusion, Belsen was partially evacuated. In the course of a meandering deportation, Lévy-Hass got separated from the train, and was liberated by the Russians in the village in which she found herself. By foot, by train, by persistence she made her way back to Jugoslavia in July 1945, and there found work with Radio Belgrade and with the new communist government. By political and national conviction, she might have made the rest of her life in Jugoslavia, but she was deeply unsettled there. Most members of her family had been killed or were in emigration; her links with pre-war, pre-Belsen life had been personal and political, not institutional. The remaining threads of continuity were finally snapped by two events: the Tito-Stalin confrontation, and the foundation of the state of Israel in 1948. These things were connected for her:

the USSR supported the establishment of Israel, while Lévy-Hass's Jugoslav friends condemned it as an imperialist adventure. Lévy-Hass seems to have been caught — not for the first time — between her nationality, her politics and her 'race'. Instead of staying trapped inside this, she embraced its contradictions and at the end of 1948 emigrated to Israel — not as a zionist or religious Jew, but as a Jewish socialist drawn to the struggle to build socialism in another country. There she joined the Israeli communist party (founded by Jews and Arabs together), and stayed a member until it split ideologically and nationally under the strains of war in the 1960s. Still she remained active on the left, as far as her poor health would allow, and in the 1970s also became involved in the new Israeli feminist movement, which she saw as a logical extension of her marxism into newly presented struggles for human emancipation.

These and other decisions and beliefs are the subject of the interview which forms an integral part of this edition of her diary. This was not the first time the diary had been published: copies in Serbo-croat and in French had been privately circulated in both Jugoslavia and Israel, and after the Eichmann trial in 1961 it appeared in somewhat larger editions in Austria, Israel and Italy. But the recent German edition by Rotbuch (1979) was the first on a large scale, and its context deserves some comment.

In the interview, it is evident that Lévy-Hass understands the principal aim of the German edition to be that of reminding the Germans that these things really happened, that the unbelievable had had its time, its place, its victims, and its perpetrators. The interviewer, however, refers to additional reasons for publication which are not made explicit in the text of their discussion. These also help to explain the decision to publish the diary in Germany in the 1970s, though they are connected less with history than with the present. The diary and interview demonstrate the difference between the official policy of the state of Israel and the European Jewish diaspora, and also that between anti-semitism and an opposition to extreme zionist nationalism — differences which are proclaimed in the very person of Hanna Lévy-Hass, the non-zionist, non-believing Israeli Jewish communist. Like Isaac Deutscher, she is a 'non-Jewish Jew', a member of an assimilated diaspora reconvened only by the imposition of a common fate during the war. These facts need emphasising at a time when national and political interests try to collapse anti-zionism and anti-semitism together, and confuse the political specificity of each. West German philo-semitism, sentimental, self-interested and self-protective by turns, illuminates neither the causes and processes of the Nazi exterminations nor the current political conflicts of Israeli and Palestinian nationalism; least of all does it address the relationship between West Germany's Nazi past and its current society and politics. Politically, that relationship has been obfuscated and suppressed, and this has been aided academically, with the persistent presentation of the Nazi regime as simply a derivation from Hitler, and a regime *sui generis*; and culturally, with the reduction of experience to commercial sentiment. As Wolfgang Pohrt has written, 'That the German past has been made socially acceptable under the trademark of the TV series "Holocaust" is proof enough that its current rediscovery is being paid for by its political neutralisation — that the birth of concern for National Socialism is nothing other than a first-class funeral'.

Such distortions are challenged by Lévy-Hass's diary and

Geisel's interview. Both elicit the continuous political meanings in her life, erected upon her commitment to a rational politics of collective socialism which has survived the astonishing convulsions of her physical life. Belsen, postwar Jugoslavia, Israel all challenged her to construct meanings and actions to bridge the space between her marxist philosophy and apparently intractable material realities. She locates that bridge precisely where it is most difficult to cross: in an assent to change which is at the same time an insistence on the struggle to gain active control of it. To say that Lévy-Hass's turbulent and tragic life symbolises a universal dilemma of her age would be to forsake politics for rhetoric. The point is to see her life as a constant exchange between the individual and the social, a process in which power and choice, unequally distributed in the social sphere, return to the individual in the shape of the possibility of analytic clarity and collective action. No doubt this is true of every life; but what the texts published here offer is the presence of a woman of exceptional self-consciousness and perceptive intensity, struggling with the danger of knowledge at the very limit of the endurable; and afterwards, not abandoning that struggle.

JANE CAPLAN

REFERENCES AND FURTHER READING

Isaac Deutscher, *The Non-Jewish Jew, and other essays* (London, 1968)

Raul Hilberg, *The Destruction of the European Jews* (New York, 1969)

Eberhard Kolb, *Bergen-Belsen. Geschichte des 'Aufenthaltsla-gers' 1943–1945* (Hanover, 1962)

Helmut Krausnick et al., *Anatomy of the SS State* (London, 1968)

Terence des Pres, *The Survior. An Anatomy of Life in the Death Camps* (New York, 1969)

Anna Pawelczynska, *Values and Violence in Auschwitz. A Sociological Analysis* (Berkeley, 1979)

Wolfgang Pohrt, *Ausverkauf. Von der Endlösung zu ihrer Alternative* (Berlin, 1980)

A BELSEN DIARY 1944 – 1945
by
Hanna Lévy-Hass

To forget is to betray
– Dolores Ibárruri
(La Pasionaria)

I

Belsen 16.8.1944. My mind is paralysed and I feel my apathy to the outside world increasing day by day. And day by day I feel less and less capable of continuing the sort of life I am leading now. If we do not achieve our goals and our expectations, if the world remains as it is, and if new patterns of human relationships do not succeed in substantially changing human nature, then I shall stand for ever condemned as an ignorant bungler, and incompetent creature on whom lies the curse of failure.

Up till now I have usually – I like to think invariably – looked for the sources of my misery and unhappiness in myself, in my own nature, my character, my origins. I have always sought to explain the inevitability of each individual's fate against a background of heredity, family influences, upbringing, childhood and other psychological factors. So I set about understanding and explaining my own life in just the same way. And it was without doubt more or less the right way.

But it has recently become ever clearer to me that one cannot look for the 'flaw' exclusively in oneself and in one's own personal existence, for to a large extent it is rooted in the world around us. Today I know with certainty that the endless days of misery, the morbid thoughts and the periods of anguish in my life have generally been the direct product of external vicissitudes, the senselessness of our present social structure and the nature of present-day man.

All this has become obvious today, even here in this camp, in the cruel oppression that unites us. I have learnt, for example, to see my own fate as intimately linked with the universal issues that underlie our international and social tensions, and to view the solution to my own problem, in the first instance, within the framework of a solution to the world's problems. I have also resolved to cease being a victim of my earlier attitudes and to escape from the grip of that helpless fatalism which brought down an inexorable, ineluctable tragedy upon me, a tragedy preordained by fate. It is obvious that my personal tragedy does derive to some extent from factors of this kind, but it is nothing fixed or prescribed, for in the general context of social and other changes my own fate is itself subject to changes from which it cannot escape.

Belsen 19.8.44. The men and women shut up in here are from various social classes but the majority of them belong to the petit bourgeoisie. There are also a few capitalists, in the true sense, with typically degenerate traits. As a rule all the inmates are selfish and have developed mean and petty habits. As a result there are perpetual conflicts and frictions, as well as rampant hypocrisy.

It is impossible to breathe in this atmosphere. The worst thing is not that these deportees have been brought here from all over the world, so that one is surrounded by twenty-five different languages – it is that there is no clear, common consciousness to unite us. We are a crowd of people of numerous different types, confined in this cramped, dusty, damp place, cruelly deprived of necessities and forced to live in the most degrading conditions, so that all human weaknesses and passions are let loose, sometimes in the most bestial of forms.

What a tragic spectacle! What shame! People united in a common misery but who can barely tolerate each other and who make their actual physical wretchedness worse by their lack of social consciousness, their intellectual blindness and the incurable maladies caused by spiritual isolation. It is an ideal breeding ground for selfish instincts, which some-times take on grotesque forms. True, it would be wrong to call these phenomena universal. But the superior qualities that one can sense in certain individuals are obscured, their moral and intellectual integrity left impotent.

Belsen 20.8.44. I feel as tired as it is possible for a human being to be, and at a distance from everything around me. My spirit aches and groans. Beauty, Truth, Love – where have they hidden themselves? What suffering it brings to think of my whole life. . . .

Belsen 22.8.44. The cramped conditions, the difficulty of keeping clean – it is all too much. When it rains, the ground turns into mud, and the insects multiply. And all the time our common enemy, the Nazi, is there, systematically irritating and provoking us. This is only the first month. In my depression I can see endless misery ahead. . . .

I ought really to have joined the partisans 'up there' in the mountains. There too, of course, we should have had our

little differences and found various anomalies – inconsisten-
cies in one man, unreliability and a lack of principles in
another. Maybe that would have been even more bitter,
even more painful to bear. But one would at least have felt
like a human being that could think, talk and act as it
wished. And one would have been surrounded by human
beings, real human being who said human things, the only
men who merit our respect today and whose words and
actions matter. Only with the partisans could I have found
the justification for my life and its real value – what I was
able, and unable, to contribute. Only there would suffering
have any meaning, human shortcomings manifest themselves and become easier to correct, men come to know
themselves and surrender themselves to a higher cause. And
if it had emerged that I were a useless person, then that too
would have been to the general advantage. All would have
become clearer, and the only thing left for me would have
been to decay like a fruit left rotting on the ground.

And why not? Such is the way of the world – though in
the depths of my soul I sense that I would not have been
doomed to failure among the partisans. Perhaps this is the
dilemma that has tormented me for so long and has landed
me in this accursed camp. At the same time it has clarified
many things both about myself and about others. And
today I can say categorically that I was meant, if not with
absolute certainty, then with a high degree of probability, to
be 'up' there with the partisans rather than in this place.
Yet this process of development has had one result I cannot
ignore – it has strengthened my convictions, so that I now
know the enemy better and recognise more clearly what
we must fight against. This knowledge was worth acquiring . . .

Belsen 23.8.44. What I have just said is not quite accurate. I had this certainty far earlier, and I did not have to wait until I was thirty, or submit to all these humiliating trials and tribulations, before acquiring it. But many others have been able to solve this vital question far more quickly and decisively. This is the terrible thing. This is why I am so dissatisfied with myself and often in a state of desperation. Will this conflict between two worlds torment me, and others like me, all our lives? Or can we hope for ultimate victory? There seems something inevitable about it all, as though it is a natural process in people whose lives have been lived under conditions similar to mine, a process that will probably repeat itself at the beginning of our new life, as it does in the world of Gorki, or of Romanov and Gladkov. These are the outward expressions of inner conflicts and destructive moral agonies, and the only way to put an end to all these morbid manifestations of the evolution of man is to fight and fight again. Yet I do not wish these effusions to be taken as a form of self-justification. One cannot justify mistakes which one has oneself been the first to admit, or deficiences which one has been the first to condemn.

Belsen 24.8.44   I am weary beyond measure and totally apathetic. What is there to add? A world disintegrating. A new and healthier world will take its place. I tremble with joy at the prospect of this new life, the approaching victory of truth and light. Many things, in books, in our actions, in our lives, will become clear. Everything will become simpler, purer, more just, and brutal situations like this will no longer find a place there.

Belsen 26.8.44. One thing here upsets me terribly, and that is to see that the men are far weaker and far less able to stand up to hardship than the women – physically and often morally as well. Unable to control themselves, they display such a lack of moral fibre that one cannot but be sorry for them. Hunger shows in their faces and movements in a far more frightening way than it does in the women.

With many of them it is either ignorance or a lack of will power that makes them incapable of controlling their desire for food. It is the same with their reaction to thirst, tiredness and similar physical strains. They cannot adapt to circumstances, and lack the strength to keep to their principles. Some of them look so miserable that they make others feel worse than they feel themselves. Some have so lost their self-discipline that in moments of extreme tension and suffering they become totally possessed by a vicious and unconcealed greed, and have not the slightest sense of identity with their fellow-victims.

Is the whole male sex like this? Surely not. If it were, how could we account for those men who continue the fight and remain strong in the face of all adversities, men able to bear suffering in silence and with dignity, men capable of restraining their instincts because they are impelled by nobler thoughts than those of food and primitive physical needs? To be sure, however they behave here is merely a natural continuation of their past. But most of them have for too long been used to filling their stomachs at will and satisfying their basest instincts without let or hindrance. For too long such men put the satisfaction of their personal desires and comforts at the centre of their lives as a matter of course, so that having to do without something or give something up seemed a major disaster, a totally inconceivable demand. Self-discipline is one of the unpleasant new realities which they have not been able to get used to: they see it as something necessary only for the others. It is a difficult, almost impossible task to touch the conscience of such people, for in this respect they have no conception of responsibility. Another, far more damaging consequence of this is that only very few behave bravely and with dignity in the face of the enemy.

Belsen 28.8.44. I have taken on the task of looking after the children. There are 110 children of various ages in our hut, ranging from three to fifteen, boys and girls. It is not easy to work without any kind of book, and I have to write subjects down on dozens and dozens of little pieces of paper, some for the little ones who can scarcely read or write, others for the older ones. They get hold of pencils and paper in whatever way they can, selling their bread ration, or doing some other kind of deal, or simply stealing from each other.

In the absence of books we sometimes just have oral classes, in which the children have to pay specially close attention. We are often interrupted by roll-calls, air-raid warnings or the appearance of various committees which remind us of visits we used to make to the zoo. 'Circumstances beyond our control', as the phrase has it, frequently hinder our work too, like the frightful din that breaks out close to our 'classroom' when the slave gangs are being hounded by the SS, or when arguments and angry scenes develop when our food is doled out.

The children are uninhibited, wild, starving. They feel their lives have taken a strange, unnatural turn, and they react instinctively, brutally. In such an atmosphere of fear and mistrust evil habits quickly spread when difficulties crop up. A small minority of the children show a certain interest in learning but the others remain indifferent. They know that the Germans have forbidden any organised education in the camp and that it is only possible to do any serious learning in secret, so they can stay away with impunity.

But there is no point in remonstrating with them. Indeed, it would be ridiculous. Any attempt at moral education is doomed to failure. The adults become irritated by the children's unruliness and sometimes call them layabouts or young criminals; they insist on meting out strict punishment as a deterrent, like beating them or taking away their bread ration – all for the sake of their own peace and quiet. When I protest, they vent their anger on what they call 'that way of teaching' – as if one could talk about 'teaching' in a situation like this, or make the children behave nicely and politely in this savage and inhuman environment, where nerves are on edge, adults fight, steal from each other and curse and swear at each other, and where everything has become defiled and dishonoured.

People have forgotten that it is more important and more effective to set a good example than to give advice and dole out punishment. Even in so-called normal circumstances the education in our schools back home, in Jugoslavia, was lacking in so many respects. How many ridiculous things went on there that were totally unsuited to the needs of the people and contrary to the spirit of the age! So often our teaching seemed irrelevant and meaningless. It started with the repressive tendency and generally unprogressive nature of the curriculum. It may have been possible, with great effort, to change a few things now and again, but in the main everything stayed as it had been. So how absurd it is to dream of some perfect form of education in a concentration camp like this.

At all events we do what we can, and sometimes the children's basic goodness asserts itself, and surprising things happen. In fact, so much strength of character do these children have that they can sometimes be made to do things we would never have thought possible.

Besides that, it is grotesque to blame the children for things of which they are the last we can consider guilty. The deep-seated sources of this wickedness cannot be eradicated by the physical punishment of its victims or by violent reaction to the effects it has caused. One must attack the roots of the evil itself. This is why I am looking so impatiently for the advent of the new age that will enable us to attack this evil at its source. And I eagerly imagine the opportunities I shall have as a teacher. How happy it would make me if my efforts were crowned with success! But perhaps I shall fail to measure up to the challenge. The same doubts persist, the same anxieties, for a large part of our nature still clings to the sick and dying world of the present and the past. . . . I can feel my fury rising against the conditions in this place, and a deep pessimism comes over me.

Belsen 29.8.44. A person is sick if he has no books. It is as though my innermost being has been destroyed. A host of wasted hours, riches lost, never to be regained, a miserable, barren life, the mind stunted and shrivelled. I meditate a great deal, and in this place of misery I have learnt many things which had hitherto passed me by. But I also think with sadness of life as it really is, this life of free men, and of all the things I have failed to learn, even here, and of all the gaps in my knowledge.

A general air of suspicion permeates the whole camp, including our own hut – a total lack of concern for the fate of others, a lack of sincerity and a sense of community. So there is hardly any exchange of ideas, or discussion about books, or any attempt to make intellectual or even normal human contact. . . .

Belsen 30.8.44. For more than a month we have all been waiting for some extraordinary event that will transform our situation overnight, because of the exciting news we have been getting about the situation at the front, in the occupied countries and in Germany itself. According to rumours that seem more or less confirmed, France is almost completely liberated. Rumania is in a state of revolt and the Russians are marching into Hungary. We even get reports of headlines in German newspapers like 'Michael of Rumania's treachery more despicable than Emanuel of Italy's' and 'Germany let down by her cowardly allies.' Even though such things seem incredible, they at least leave us with a sense of satisfaction. Optimists suddenly appear, making prognostications and counting the days to freedom. We all feel the end approaching and are gripped willy-nilly by a mad delusion that all will soon be over.

Yet the camp routine has become worse, become stricter, which creates in the prisoners a nervous tension, a sense of desperation. The persecution and the sense of shame become even more oppressive as the end draws nigh.

The men in the labour gangs outside are brutally treated. The German savages keep to their favourite methods, savagely beating the prisoners and showering them with hysterical abuse. They force them into the most humiliating situations, like shuffling along on their knees or pulling carts at the double, blows raining down on them the whole time. Sometimes the Nazis arrange a furious bicycle race among themselves and make the prisoners run behind: if, as always happens, one of them fails to show the requisite enthusiasm and collapses in exhaustion, the German heroes demonstrate their power by withdrawing the offender's bread ration or putting him in solitary confinement. The whole time the prisoners are subjected to a ceaseless barrage of the crudest insults and most violent abuse, so that one begins to doubt whether, even in their private lives, these Nazis are still capable of talking quietly and behaving like human beings.

They never stop humiliating and insulting the Jews, although it must gradually be dawning on them that their own end is near. They welcome any chance to show their contempt. The roll-call, for instance – all the prisoners have to fall in every morning on the parade ground and stand to attention in ranks of five to be counted – gives them ample opportunity to show their hatred.

This daily roll-call takes at least two or three hours, and often, almost every other day, they make it last five or six hours, sometimes even a whole day, whatever the weather, under some pretext or other, or because of something that has happened. Apart from these regular roll-calls we are often ordered to fall in at other times of the day as well, in order to listen to some ridiculous announcement. Two or three officers take these roll-calls, and anyone who dares to move and so disturb the ranks is severely dealt with. It is an agonising scene, especially the sight of old men and women, maybe from southern Jugoslavia, standing in front of one of these vicious Prussian upstarts, shivering with cold and fear. For years they have stood for a life of decency and moderation, working hard and showing a traditional respect for their fellow-men; now all they are expected to do is stand to attention in front of these rabid criminals who spit in their faces and trample on their spirit and every aspect of their dignity.

Then there are the children. They know no joy, only fear, these poor, humiliated little creatures who are made to stand to attention for hours, trembling in fright, waiting blankly for what is to happen next. Covering their heads with some piece of rag, they cling to the adults in search of protection from cold and fear, looking feverishly around with wide-open eyes, like hounded beasts.

The brutal German officers survey the scene with cold-blooded contempt. 'Attention!' they shout. A deathly silence settles over the crowd. They announce that one or other of the prisoners is to be put in solitary confinement or sent to another, harsher camp for having taken a few potatoes from the galley or stolen a pair of shoes from the store, or some such reason. The offender is then brought into the middle of the square and made to turn round in front of all of us. It is like a circus, with rows and rows of prisoners on the outside, thousands of human shadows, and the 'offenders' in the middle, each with his little pack on his back. They stand there at attention, mocked and shouted at, waiting to be led away at the end of the performance.

The onlookers are made to learn that if they follow the example of these 'offenders', the same or a worse fate awaits them. But if they are satisfied with your work, and you show yourself enthusiastic and cooperative, hurrying obediently from one place to another, clicking your heels at every opportunity and saying 'Certainly, Herr Oberscharführer!' or 'Whatever you say, Sir!' on all possible occasions – and, sad to say, there are enough such people – then you will receive a 'bonus', such as an extra bread ration or an extra portion of turnip soup. In a word: this is the perfect institution for teaching 'respect' – an institution where men are starved and cramped together like animals, a school for forced labour, for wretched men and women and uncontrollable children, whose spirit has already been crushed.

Belsen 31.8.44. The JPA (Jewish Press Agency), a remarkable organisation that circulates information among the prisoners, has announced that the Germans intend to evacuate our camp in a hurry because they need it for military purposes (Belsen lies between Hamburg, Hanover and Bremen, in the administrative *Bezirk* of Celle; the nearest town of any size is Lüneburg). Word has it that we are to be transported elsewhere. Meanwhile endless convoys continue to arrive with fresh batches of prisoners, day and night. As our numbers grow, so does our misery. Are we going to be evacuated or not? Who knows? Uncertainty reigns wherever we are, and we are utterly in their power.

There is no roll-call this morning. Something is going on in the next compound (criminals and political prisoners): some are being taken away, or new ones are arriving. Or perhaps a new camp commandant is suddenly going to arrive, or new guards. Who knows? The main thing is that there is no roll-call. That means there will be one twice as long this afternoon or tomorrow.

Belsen 1.9.44. The roll-call really did last twice as long as usual. Maybe one of the children came late or something. We are so often left to stand in the square for hours that we have given up trying to understand why – as though there really were a reason.

An autumn day, dull, damp, continuous drizzle, with a

strong wind like our *koshava* in Jugoslavia, but stronger. At
roll-call this morning we were frozen to the marrow.

The whole day was spent in replacing two-tier bunks by
three-tier. We only managed to do a third of the hut, which
means it will take us at least two or three more days. The
reason given was that it made space for the table and left us
more room to move. But this was only an excuse, and in the
event we had to find room for a number of older children
between fourteen and sixteen who had previously not had
their own bunks. As a result we are more cramped than
ever, with less room to sleep, less air to breathe and no extra
room to move about. It is impossible to move on these
three-tier bunks, still less to sit on them. There is just
enough space to crawl on to them at night, provided one
bends enough and does not move one's body too much.

There is naturally much more walking to and fro between these new beds than before. The narrowness is
enough to drive one mad – shouts, groans, tramping backwards and forwards, endless quarrelling, a din like an
inferno, with people continually shuffling about carrying
palliasses, soup bowls and left-over scraps of food affection-
ately laid out on some smelly cloth. Others walk around the
whole time with boards, odd rags and damp clothes, to the
accompaniment of despairing cries and children weeping.
Everything is covered in dust; straw lies all over the floor,
mixed with garbage and excrement, and the stench is indescribable.

Arguments are inevitable, especially among the women,
when beds are allocated and the washing has to be done.
Each one regards herself as a particular object of resentment, the victim of some particular injustice, blind to the
fact that the others are just as distressed. Here we are all

slaves and are deliberately piled on top of each other without enough air to breathe. They deliberately watch us squabbling and arguing and swearing at each other, for they are out to make our lives intolerable and turn us into animals, so as to be able to jibe at us, humiliate us and torment us all the more easily. The beasts. And since they have suddenly cut off the water, it has become even worse.

I stand next to my bed, regard the whole scene and ponder. Others force me away, pushing me from one side to the other. Refuse all over the floor and cries ringing out. I just do not know where to sit and where to go so as not to be in other people's way – or in my own way. I do not know where to put myself.

Yesterday the Dutch Jews here celebrated their beloved Queen's birthday. They even acted a play for the children. However could they think of such a thing at a time like this? I can hardly believe my eyes when I see them in their Sunday best. When they were deported they were not stripped of everything by the Germans, as we were. Shall we ever learn why? Anyway, our Dutchmen are very smartly dressed as they walk around. Two youngsters catch my eye in particular, wearing fresh white collars and ties. They really are! A touching occasion, this royal birthday – really moving.

Belsen 4.9.44. Our hut is like a madhouse. Only a few are capable of controlling themselves. The slightest incident leads to vicious arguments, threats, insults and abuse. Everyone is irritable, on edge, waiting to be provoked, ready to assume a personal animosity on the part of the next person. Everyone's mind is full of distrust, suspicion and deceitfulness. It makes one shudder.

A tragedy, O what a tragedy! Fright, hunger and abject fear fill their unhappy faces, especially at mealtimes. Everyone has somehow to pick up the ladle and get his bowl two-thirds full, until the pot is completely empty. Those in the crowd who are afraid they will not get their ration look desperate and begin to cry, seized with panic lest the pot should only be half-full. And the whole time this feverish struggle for a plate of watery turnip soup is going on, people are pushing their way backwards and forwards down the narrow gangways between the bunks, shouting and screaming. Chamber pots, empty and full, are ceaselessly being carried from one end of the hut to the other for the children and the sick.

In the midst of this pandemonium, as soup, smells and excrement pass by, as brooms send up clouds of dust, as children weep and adults scream, the shameless 'dealers' make their incessant rounds, pestering their equally unhappy 'customers' to exchange some rags for bread, or bread for cigarettes, or vice versa. It is a strange form of trade, accompanied by never-ending discussions and negotiations.

A wailing, stinking scene of endless misery, turned into a disgusting public spectacle. It is exactly what the Nazis intended – to humiliate us and reduce us to animals, to drive us out of our minds, to extinquish even the faintest memory we might still have that we were once human beings.

Belsen 6.9.44. They are rounding up their slave labour again, driving them out of the huts, kicking and punching them and hitting them with cudgels. 'Everybody outside!' Men, women, young and old, children, the healthy and the sick – everybody. 'Fall in!' We form rows of five. They count us like cattle – though cattle have never been treated with such contempt and abuse as we are. 'Forward, march!' – and the new gang is led away. It is repulsive. Can one find anyone in the world whose cruelty and wickedness can be set beside that of these Nazi beasts, or anything that can be compared with the way they are destroying human beings physically and morally? These brutes!

Not far from here, some five or six hundred yards away, we can clearly make out an isolated little camp surrounded by barbed wire. A few hundred Hungarian Jews are being held there. But we are not allowed to go there. Rumour has it that they get food parcels from abroad. The Germans call it a 'special' camp. 'For Jews?' we ask. 'Yes.' 'Why is it "special"?' 'Because they have special papers,' comes the reply. Strange.

II

Belsen 8.9.44. I would rather not look at it any more and put it all out of my mind. But I find I cannot. A few weeks ago I tried in vain to take no heed of what was happening around me. Today I can realise that my life cannot be separated from life in the camp, and that for better or for worse we are united by a common fate to share a common misery.

Even if I wrote and wrote, page after page, I could never describe all the aspects of our wretchedness, never convey all the cruel details of our lives. And think only of the difficulty of tracing the course of each one of these tragic lives, their earlier misfortunes, the individual calamities that have issued in this common tragedy, the links of the curse that binds us. I would never finish. The range of human suffering is boundless, and unfathomable the depths of the human soul in moments of torture and terror. It would be a waste of effort to try to describe it all. It lies far beyond my competence.

Watching the despairing agony of the mass of prisoners, I have more than once imagined I was looking at Dante's Inferno – but not for the pleasure of indulging in literary associations, for the only visions that my mind could absorb were the images of hell that had established themselves in my imagination over the years. It was the only picture in my mind, the only memory I could recall.

The horrors which confront us and which we are forced to endure are so great that the mind is paralysed and totally unable to respond to anything not directly connected with them. So at this moment I can only recall the most recent past – the terrible journey to this place. Fifteen days in cattle trucks, forty, sixty of us crammed into each – men, women, the aged, children. Locked in, without air, without light, without food, without water. Stifling, suffocating, parched with thirst, everywhere filth, sweat, foul odours and fumes.

Only twice during these two weeks were we given a little water to drink and some canned food. On our way through Czechoslovakia we had what they called 'a stroke of luck': the Czech Red Cross served us with hot soup. We were beside ourselves with joy. Then we were given water. It is impossible to describe the expression on the Czechs' faces as they watched us fighting for every drop. Who knows what they saw in our eyes and the way we looked?

The terrible journey continued. The Germans refused to open the trucks, even to let us relieve ourselves. Only three times during the whole journey were we allowed to get out for this purpose. And it was so vile and humiliating that the thought of it still makes me blush. The train stopped in beautiful countryside, in the middle of wide, open fields, We were in pain. The Nazi soldiers stood close by and brazenly watched us, ordering us to hurry up, holding their rifles at the ready and 'guarding' us.

And all the while they sadistically leered and swore at us, cursing those who were so sick, so exhausted through lack of food and drink, so pitifully self-conscious that they could not finish what they were doing. Not once did I see on the face of any of these soldiers the slightest sign of normal human feeling, the faintest hint of sympathy, let alone of shame or embarrassment at being made to behave like this. Their faces were utterly inhuman.

As the train passed through villages at night time it was fired on by partisans or strafed by a hail of machine-gun bullets from aircraft. There was one air-raid warning after another. The Germans rushed out of the train and took cover, while we stayed locked up in the trucks, panic-stricken, a sitting target. Huddled together in the darkness, the children almost deafened us with their screams, the women moaned and wailed, the men argued over a bit of space for themselves. Even in this state of hysterical fear and despair they did not stop squabbling and swearing at each other. We had a mad desire to stretch out but could not; sleep was out of the question, and even breathing was an effort. It was hell.

When we finally reached our destination, without having the slightest idea where we were, and crawled out of our holes, we felt like wild animals that had just escaped being killed. Then began the sombre march along the seemingly endless road to the camp at Belsen, as we dragged ourselves along, exhausted, haggard, starving, the glint of fever in our eyes, covered in dust and sweat, weighed down by the few pitiful possessions we had been allowed to keep. Ghastly human shadows threading their slow, silent way down an unknown path. Villagers, women in pretty summer frocks, men on bicycles and on foot, all relaxed, well groomed and well dressed, wearing the untroubled look of people leading a 'normal' life, paused for a moment and looked at us with curiosity. But they did not shed a scrap of their indifference. And the hordes of soldiers strode beside the column with their rifles, hitting out at anyone who turned round or dared to slow down a little.

This was the moment when our tortured spirits began to store up the memories of all the indignity and abuse that were to grow into a mountain of anguish.

Belsen 17.9.44. My pain and misery are suffocating me. So is my hate. It is a happy man who does not suffer when he hates, but that is beyond me. Tears keep filling my eyes – tears of shame and rage. A poisoned spirit is so bitter. These tears of shame and rage are choking me. I am being driven out of my mind by emotions that clamour for expression but are improperly and brutally repressed. I am so afraid of the time when I shall recall these emotions. My body is convulsed by sobs as I think of the injustice and wretchedness in the world, the injustice and wretchedness in myself, and my mind begins to break up.

Belsen 25.9.44. New huts are being built. For whom? Nobody knows. But we can guess. There is more talk of big loads of prisoners being expected in the camp. The work is being carried out with feverish haste, new huts being put up in almost all the spaces between the old ones. Everyone has to work at it. Slave gangs being rounded up, sudden swoops by the Nazis, beatings, swearing – the same pattern over and over.

In retaliation against acts of sabotage the Germans have reduced our daily bread ration. We are at the end of our tether, utterly exhausted through malnutrition and forced labour, and those who smoke are suffering through having no cigarettes. I watch some of them collecting the stubs that the Germans have thrown away on the square or going to the garbage cans outside the galleys to look for mouldy left-overs.

The situation inside the huts is just as bad. We are all suffering the pangs of starvation. An unidentified epidemic is running through the camp, striking the women and children in particular. It lasts two or three weeks and takes the form of a continuous high temperature, with fainting fits, exhaustion and total loss of appetite. There is no marked pain. The doctors call it 'camp fever', paratyphoid or some such name, and claim that the symptoms do not permit any definite diagnosis. There is a sick man or woman in almost every other bunk.

Then there are the abscesses and running sores caused by malnutrition and the bugs; suppurating ulcers, boils, contusions, oedemas, spasms and all kinds of infection – these are everyday occurrences. Sometimes there are a few drugs or medicines; more often there are none. There is clearly no question of giving the sick medical treatment, real medical treatment. Either they will get better if their powers of resistance are strong enough, or they will be left to die. The whim of fate decides.

In addition, for three-quarters of the time there is no water in the taps, for no good reason. The excuse is that the water is needed for the central showers, but it is over two months since we were taken to have a bath.

It immediately strikes us how strange it is that the water should be cut off just at the time when epidemics are spreading and we need more water to try and cope with our lamentable situation. The very thing we require for cleanliness and the elementary demands of hygiene is the very thing we are denied.

Heedless of all that happens, autumn moves onwards. The grim prospect of a terrible winter makes us shiver. Then there is the rain and mud. The whole day the air is full of the sound of hammering and the creaking of timber as the construction work goes on and new huts are erected.

Belsen 11.10.44. True, everything is relative. . . . Each prisoner will have his own tale to tell about this dreadful place. And there will be 'truths' in these tales – different, variable, relative truths. It all depends on one's own subjective viewpoint, on the position from which one makes one's observations, on one's own attitude towards this whole spectacle.

I have noticed strange things in the last few days. Between six hundred and eight hundred of the 7,000 who live in our block are employed in various interior and exterior building jobs. These people have weak consciences, are always ready to compromise and adapt to what is required of them, and this opportunistic attitude gains them exceptional privileges. They are given top quality clothes and huge quantities of food. They get everything they need, even more, or are given the opportunity to procure it. As a result they have long since forgotten how the others suffer. Spoilt by the unnatural abundance in which they live, they are no longer aware of those who are dying of starvation around them and crying out for a crust of bread. Some of them have cast off all scruples and lost all sense of moral value. Happy at being allowed to eat and stay alive, they are tireless in their praise of this good-hearted German or that. Nor are they ashamed to evolve theories that the Germans are only vulgar and brutal because so many of our people do not know how to work properly, and are inefficient, clumsy and apathetic. 'That sort of thing gets their goat,' they say. 'They find it sickening, and justifiably so. You must understand that. For in fact the Germans behave very correctly, just as one should do towards intelligent and honest workers. People like this they actually treat very kindly . . .'

A sad way of justifying the situation but an unhappily frequent one, especially among those who are regarded as 'respectable' and 'responsible', or as 'intellectuals'. Take R., an engineer, who is a perfect example – there is just no point in arguing with him. He is no ignoramus. He knows full well that the Germans only behave properly and relatively humanely towards those who have made up their minds to identify themselves with Nazi policies and methods in word and deed. And he knows it is very dubious whether the Nazis really trust such people, because they have been brought up in a tradition of mad chauvinism and absolute contempt for their fellow-men. He is also fully aware, this sorry creature, that the Germans are far from behaving properly towards those who adopt a detached, passive attitude in order to give open expression to their awareness of being deportees and slaves, and in this way make it clear that the Germans are their enemies and nothing but their enemies. The Germans are obviously not going to be indulgent towards prisoners like these.

The 'lucky ones' who have managed to gain special privileges always employ the classic arguments of defeatists and opportunists. 'At the moment', they say, 'the main thing is to save one's skin and somehow emerge safe and sound, come what may. We'll keep our thoughts to ourselves.' And all the while they exploit their privileges for the benefit of themselves and those close to them. These characters, who often declare their Germanophile sympathies quite openly and brazenly, can be found everywhere – in the food stores, the clothes lockers, inside and outside the camp workshops, at the railway station, in the kitchens of the SS and the other military units, and in camp kitchens 1 and 2.

They try to convince us that the life of plenty that they enjoy does no harm to the other prisoners or does not affect their interests and basic rights in any way. They make out that their well-being has in no way been bought at the price of the misery of the non-privileged, the rest of the starving inmates of the camp. Nothing of the kind, they say – it's just their good fortune.

But it remains a fact that they scarcely concern themselves at all with what goes on inside the bug-ridden huts that reek of putrefaction, of fever, of starvation and death, not to mention the mental agony. They shut their eyes and ears to everything that goes on and have not the slightest idea of the real situation. Indeed, they admit it themselves. Most of them have their own huts, which are relatively clean and comfortable, and have built their own little world. No wonder the sound of laughter and merriment and singing can be heard coming from there. They return from their work well-fed and in good spirits. They are particular about their dress and organise concerts, binges, boozing-parties and other social gatherings. The women wear smart clothes, their beds are sweetly scented and their rooms are tastefully decorated. They tell jokes and indulge in amorous adventures. And of course they do not forget their superiors. They share their possessions with those in charge of the huts, who do not go out to work and appear on the surface to have official links with the Germans. They also have a less strict routine of their own to conform to. So they laugh and flirt, those who belong to this gang, and pretend it is all so innocent. We only want to stay alive, they say: and after all, who knows how we shall end up?

People like this, of course, will give a quite different account of the camp, of the Germans and of everything that has gone on. Some will even take pleasant memories with them, memories of an enjoyable time, of the 'kindness' of the Germans, of a vague feeling of happiness and of having been 'lucky'. It is all so relative, so relative.

Belsen 17.10.44. Something has happened in the next part of the camp. There are Polish women interned there, though we are not sure whether they are political prisoners or Jews. We know only that they are treated worse than we are. A number of them are kept in close custody. Today they apparently took action and rebelled – arranged a demonstration, perhaps, according to the rumours that reached us. Suddenly everyone was ordered back into the huts. The labour gangs came back early, and in the galleys orders were given for the fires to be put out and the kitchen staff sent away. The big gates separating our compounds from the rest of the camp were closed. We were terror-stricken and reduced to complete silence.

What came of the revolt by these women, we shall never know for certain. But it is clear that the Germans have 'restored order' in their usual way and committed fresh atrocities. Smoke comes continuously from the crematorium, plain for all to see.

Behind the compound in which we are crushed together there stretch row upon row of huts in every direction, as far as the eye can see, in which criminals and political prisoners are housed. There are also masses of women and children there, imprisoned under every conceivable pretext, 50,000 to 60,000 of them, a world in themselves.

Every day columns of fresh prisoners tramp along the roads that pass between the compounds, an army of unhappy creatures being led to forced labour, already victims of hunger and torture, A few hundred of them are accommodated close by, some hundred yards away, behind the barbed wire. Sorely though we would, we dare not approach them and talk to them, lest the Germans should shoot at us, fearing we would tell each other about the terrible things that have been going on. And the Germans *are* afraid of us, fearful of us humans whom they have turned into a dull, degraded mass of apathetic beasts. Proof? – Everything that has happened today.

Belsen 18.10.44. Among the bodies brought out of the hospital today – the 'hospital' is a hut like all the others – were three from our hut. One of these three was a girl of fourteen. Before the war she had been a healthy, well-developed, pretty little girl. In the prison at Podgorica she caught influenza, which quickly turned into tuberculosis. When we arrived in this camp four months ago, she was already at death's door. We watched her getting weaker and weaker day by day. Her suffering reached its climax in these last few days: she was incapable of making even the slightest movement. Her mother was quiet, resigned and made no fuss. She has two other daughters, younger, very pretty, but reduced by starvation to mere shadows. Young bodies need nourishment and have to develop, otherwise they are like saplings that wither and die.

Their father disappeared two years ago, taken away by the Ustasa.* Now they have lost their elder sister. This morning we saw her young body – so thin, so tiny. Just a few lifeless bones, covered with one of the grey, threadbare camp blankets. She was laid out on two old, narrow benches in a kind of laboratory. Above her body, close to her head, was a rack with dirty test tubes in it. A small, bare window looked out on to the grey barbed-wire fence, behind which stood more rows of bleak, grey huts. And beyond this – nothing, a cold, dark, foggy void, the rain-drenched line of the northern horizon, desolate, leaden.

In order to make it seem like a burial, we were allowed to follow the pitiful wooden coffin for some thirty yards, as far as the main gate of the camp. Part of the wire entanglement was moved to one side and the body passed through, alone, on a cart. It was the child's passage to freedom. She had died one hour after midnight. By now the flames must have consumed her.

Belsen 20.10.44. This morning it was the turn of a little old woman to die in the hut, close to my bunk. Her family wept a while, then we watched as the body was taken out. Another life is over and will soon be forgotten. We have become coarsened. Each one of us has become absorbed in his own

---

*The Croatian fascist organisation which collaborated with the Germans during the occupation of Jugoslavia 1941–44 [Transl.]

unhappiness, but at the same time the nature of our common misery becomes ever more apparent.

There have been some cases of brain disorder, a form of meningitis. The ravages of the fever epidemic continue unabated. The little children have their own particular ailments. A charming, tiny little girl of four has been in bed for five weeks with attacks of fever. Her body is covered in boils, and when her mother sits down on the side of her bunk, her head droops on to her shoulder, and she hasn't the strength to hold it up. Her lovely big eyes glisten in her haggard face and she surveys the scene around her with a sane and intelligent, albeit resigned gaze. And when they take her clothes off, there is only a skeleton to be seen. Yet she is still alive – she breathes, she suffers, she lies there in silence. There is no weeping or screaming; she is too weak for that. This morning they lanced her boils and the pus ran out in streams. For a moment she sobbed gently, then lay still and motionless again. A little martyr, a tragic symbol of misery and resignation.

Belsen 22.10.44. There was great agitation in our hut last week. As I noted before, suspicion and intolerance are widespread. In addition the contact that the prisoners have with each other tends to take on unpleasant and aggravating forms, with cunning, deceit and corruption. Those gifted with a certain 'ingenuity' and 'practical intelligence', or who curry favour with the Germans – which comes to the same thing – make sure that they will derive the benefits from any situation at the expense of the other prisoners. All those who take an unscrupulous and unprincipled attitude towards their fellow-men in general behave in this way.

This state of affairs starts at the top with the 'Senior Jew', as he is called, who is our representative in dealings with the Germans; then come his associates, who carry out the various tasks of the camp 'elite', and finally those in charge of the huts, together with their helpers and cronies. This creates a caste system in the camp: one group suffers, starves, is sick and dies, condemned to hard labour, cruelly beaten and maltreated the whole time, while the other lives in comparative comfort, well-fed, well-treated and given advantages at the expense of the others, as a result of which they gradually lose all awareness of a common fate and all feeling of brotherhood.

Initially I confined myself just to observing all this and remained 'neutral', since I felt powerless to intervene. But since then the systematic stealing and cheating, the abuses and the corruption have all reached an intolerable pitch in our hut, where conditions are a mirror of the situation in the camp as a whole. So mean, so crude and so repulsive are the ways in which all this intrigue is carried on that it fills me with disgust. It is now no longer a secret that large quantities of food intended for our hut, and in particular much of the daily soup ration, regularly and mysteriously disappear. An undisguised and flourishing trade goes on, with a system of things to buy and sell, and those who carry on this trade deal in goods that for us belong to the world of make-believe – things like silk stockings, rings, jewellery, fur coats, shoes, sophisticated toilet goods and so on. They also deal in tasty bowls of soup, specially prepared, and all kinds of appetising food, the sight of which makes us feel quite dizzy. These things are continually passing to and fro completely openly, forcing the restless ranks of starving and dying prisoners to watch what is going on. The whole atmosphere in the hut has been poisoned. Everyone is filled with resentment, jealousy and suspicion of everyone else, both with and without reason.

The hut is divided into two parts, one for men, the other for women and children, though the division is not all that strictly observed. The men show their distrust of each other in sudden outbursts of personal hatred, with curses and threats like 'Shove off, you crook, or I'll show you!' and so on. Sometimes a thief answers back, sometimes not. Or, as very frequently happens, he succeeds in corrupting his adversaries as well. To put a stop to these disgraceful goings-on would require a common sense of determination and purpose. But that is not our strong point. In the women's section the position is the same, or almost the same. Sometimes it is noisier, with hysterical outbursts, moaning and cursing, but nobody takes steps to do anything effective about it. At the same time the women do on occasion reveal signs of a more practical and more community-minded attitude, chiefly for the sake of the children. They steel themselves to find ways of remedying the situation and show real courage, even prepared, if necessary, to make sacrifices.

Last Saturday a number of them could be seen excitedly discussing something among themselves. Then they approached me and asked me to take charge of the matter. This marked the beginning of a fight which started on Saturday evening and lasted the entire week. Ultimately we emerged as the victors, to our general satisfaction. This was how it happened.

To start with we held an improvised meeting by my bunk and decided to demand an explanation in the name of the 120 women in my section as to how Frau R., who was in charge of the section, distributed the food. She protested and claimed she was honest. We then told her that, in order to remove any hint of suspicion, all she needed to do was to agree to allow a few of our representatives to assist in distributing the food and thus carry out the check that all the women had demanded. The woman in question – who happened to be the wife of the overseer in charge of the hut but was not a forceful person – was cornered and had no alternative but to give way to the wishes of the majority.

We then went further and demanded that the extra helping of soup which was taken out of our own ration and given to those who distributed the food, should be stopped. All that these characters, six to eight of them, who were relieved of all outside work, had to do, was to fetch eight or ten containers from the galley every day and take them back there after the soup had been distributed. We insisted that their unfair privileges be taken away, for a variety of reasons. The hundreds of unprivileged prisoners sent out in the forced labour gangs, who had to endure indescribable cruelties at the hands of the Nazi soldiers for ten or twelve hours every day, received no extra rations and no help from the rest of the prisoners, and knew that they could not expect it. Yet while pretending just to fetch their extra ration, these despicable characters who collected the soup used their arbitrary power to perpetrate all kinds of tricks and dodges without letting the others see what they were up to.

We then decided not to allow these women to have any extra rations or special rights at all. If they did not dole out the food 'free', we determined to get the fittest of our number to take over the work themselves, so as to guarantee that we all received our fair share. These two decisions were put into effect the very next day, a Sunday, to the eager interest of all the inmates of the hut.

The plan was perfect. But suddenly the overseer of the hut, who had formerly been the official representative of the Swedish match monopoly in Jugoslavia, and was also the husband of Frau R., began to sense that something was afoot. So he sought the help of his cronies, in particular his immediate deputy – an extremely cunning and dangerous type, easily corrupted, but with a lively, albeit crude mind – to prevent us in every conceivable way from carrying out our plan. We were fully aware that the system we had worked out was unwelcome to those in charge because it raised the prospect of a still more radical reorganisation of the hut. Our opponents' viciousness and craftiness knew no bounds, as they systematically set about undermining our position, laying all kinds of traps for us. But we did not give way. The women supported me courageously and without reservation, and we managed to forestall every new move our enemy was plotting.

Suddenly I felt an extraordinary sense of strength, of confidence and determination. I was elated. Nothing could intimidate me. I did not blind myself to the fact that the people I was fighting were obviously stronger than I, since they had the Nazis on their side; moreover they could at any moment have informed the German camp authorities of the affair. But we kept our courage up. The justice of our case and the suffering of the mass of the prisoners gave us strength and confidence. And when our enemies realised that we were to be taken seriously, that we were determined to fight to the end, not even fearing solitary confinement, that we distributed the food fairly and honestly (they made us get up before dawn, while the frost was still on the ground, making out that otherwise the soup containers would be stolen by people from other compounds, and similar stories) – in short, when they realised that we knew what we wanted, then something happened that showed the overseer in his true colours.

One morning he suddenly forced his way into the women's section and savagely announced (he is far from being a hero: he cries when he is hungry, the weakling) that 'petticoat rule' was to be abolished from now on, and that he would not tolerate any independent initiatives or 'Soviet-style republics' in his hut. The women replied that they would continue to do what they considered beneficial to the community and what the community had in fact already agreed upon. They did not need a dictatorship, they said, on top of the already difficult conditions, and refused to submit to yet another form of tyranny; finally, if their activity were broken up by force, they and their children would go on hunger strike.

As a result of this, and above all under pressure from his even craftier companions, who were afraid the affair might lead to the discovery that other, even more involved and more dubious machinations were going on behind the scenes, the overseer abruptly changed his tone and gave way to our demands. So we were able to mark up two official victories. Firstly, those who distributed the food would not get any favours for it but simply do their job in accordance with the principle of equal reward for equal work and suffering. Secondly, the food should be distributed fairly and openly, so that every one of the 120 women could see exactly where each portion went. Anything left over at the end of a meal should be given out by rota. A team was formed to supervise the new scheme, lists of names were drawn up, each one was given a number, and so on.

This event acquired great importance for me, in that it taught me the valuable lesson that men of dubious character and conscience are not as strong as they try to make out, and that it is possible to get the better of them in an open fight. I also discovered that I still had the capacity to keep my sense of purpose and adopt the most suitable means of achieving it. My brain has not become hopelessly dulled and numbed: I can easily arouse myself from my stupor and still feel enough strength and vigour to fight for a just cause. And the knowledge I have gained in recent years about life and about human character has borne fruit. In short, I discovered that I had become stronger, maturer and more self-confident than before. I also learned a lot of useful details about how to carry on the fight – little points, but of considerable tactical importance, like the need for wariness and patience, and the necessity of thinking a proposal over from all points of view before saying anything. In dealing with the Germans one must remain calm and determined; once a decision has been made, it must be carried out according to plan. This is also the best method of causing confusion among the Germans and making them give ground, especially since their much-vaunted strength is mere sham.

Something else I learned, something that must never be overlooked, is that in any struggle one must always expect to come across some irritating obstruction, caused by weak and petty-minded people of no imagination. Such people are incapable not only of seeing a common social task through to the end but even of understanding what is at stake, and are always ready to sow the seeds of confusion and distrust in the minds of others, thus obstructing the course of events. Most of them are crude, peevish, small-minded creatures who refuse to understand or agree to anything unless it will be of direct personal benefit to themselves. They will sometimes wax indignant over the corrupt conditions but only out of jealousy, and if they are allowed to take advantage of the corruption, they are prepared to keep quiet about it. Moral depravity of this kind is the perfect breeding-ground for reactionary elements in a society.

Belsen 23.10.44 According to news that reaches us from time to time, a considerable number of places back home appear to have been liberated. We have a desperate longing to go home to where people can move and go about their daily work without hindrance. Their spirits too will have been liberated, while we, imprisoned behind barbed wire, are condemned to an inhuman existence.

Belsen 23.10.44 The air-raid alarm sounds every evening at 6.30, so that the evening and the whole of the night is spent in darkness. When the labour gangs come back to the camp, the men have to grope their way to their bunks in the huts and eat their humble meal in pitch blackness. The darkness puts us even more on edge: we knock into each other, and the children shriek in their fear and anxiety. People shout out without seeing each other and bellow from one end of the hut to the other. Thieves take advantage of the situation to steal bread, the principal form of currency in the camp and the only thing that keeps us alive, if only for a little while.

This fight for bread, for the tiniest crumb, the fear of losing it or being robbed of it, whether by the thieves in our own midst or by the Germans, who sometimes amuse themselves by leaving us without our basic ration for a few days – this has become the central and most pressing problem in our lives, touching each and every one of us. The ration gets smaller and smaller from week to week. Today, measured literally by the millimetre, it amounts to just 3.5 cm. The sight of it makes us tremble as though it were a nugget of gold. Carefully and devotedly we cut it into pieces one or two millimetres thick. To have this ration stolen, or to have one or two days ration forfeited for some reason or other – or for no reason at all – amounts to a disaster.

Yet in spite of all this, in spite of the eerie darkness, the deafening noise and the danger of being robbed, we all feel a sense of satisfaction when the air-raid siren goes. First there is what I would call a sort of carefree indifference towards the possibility of being attacked by the Allied air forces. Then we calculate that, although it is not impossible, they will hardly bomb the huts in which the prisoners are kept. And beyond this, the siren is the only link we have with the outside world, the only thing that sustains our hopes. . . .

This morning the weather was clear and icy. The roofs of the huts were covered with a heavy frost, and the puddles in the yard are frozen. It will soon be November. We still have hopes. The development of world events favours our cause – of that there can be no doubt.

I devote myself regularly to the children. I feel very clearly that our 'school' has become an indispensable part of their existence, the only influence that keeps their spiritual lives cheerful and refreshed. The great majority of them are enthusiastic to learn and have the will to make up for the time they have lost. When I call them to come, they respond with shouts of joy and shout 'Hurrah!' Then the ablest among them clear a corner in the hut so that we can start, and they gather round me, their wonderful faces filled with delight but also with attentiveness and concentration.

On the days when they are prevented from having their instruction, their mood changes. They become bored and irritated, because the only thing left for them to do is to feel how hungry they are. It is indeed a tragic state of affairs when children at the age when both body and mind clamour to develop are made to waste their lives in forced mental and physical idleness under humiliating conditions of mass slavery, while their powers become stunted and withered. This is why I try as often as I can to make them learn something. With the youngest this happens almost involuntarily, and they have grown so attached to me that I can hardly free myself from them.

The older children are now coming to me as well, for Professor K. is sick and the other 'teachers' are utterly disinterested. Teaching these older children has a quality of its own. They particularly enjoy discussing with me various questions about life, which enables me to bring them into contact with ideas that I find especially valuable. One day, for instance, I gave them a poem by Verhaeren called *'L'effort'*, which I had happened to find and had translated into Serbian, and asked them to comment on it. The simplicity of the description of human work in this poem aroused a keen interest in all of them. Quite spontaneously they began to tell what they knew about the various occupations, and bit by bit I worked them round to describing the values that are created by labour, the role of the workers in society, in the exploitation of the world's natural wealth, in industrial production and so on. From this I led them on to grasp the close link that exists between the evolution of civilisa-

tion on the one hand and the working–class movement and
the consciousness of the working class on the other. Thanks
to the fact that a large number of my pupils came from the
labouring classes, such as the families of small peasants and
tradesmen from southern Jugoslavia (Kossovo and
Metohija), I was able to give the discussions a practical slant
and help the children to acquire knowledge based on their
own experience.

The food distribution is still in my hands, as had been
agreed. But it becomes more and more obvious to me that it
is difficult, indeed illusory, to think that one can make any
serious and lasting impression in such terrible conditions,
where people form an impersonal mass and are constantly
at odds with each other. Moreover I must confess that the
meanness and craftiness of these evil, corrupt beings who
fight like wild beasts to save their own skins by endangering
the lives of hundreds of their fellows, is something that lies
beyond my comprehension. Confronted with so much
baseness and corruption, I do not feel able to bear the
burden alone.

Belsen 6 November 44 A further huge convoy of prisoners
has arrived in the last few days, 1700 women of various
nationalities, most of them of Jewish descent. They have
come from Auschwitz. According to rumours circulating
here, the camp at Auschwitz has been completely, or almost
completely, wiped out, and these women are some of the
few survivors. A number of them come from northern
Jugoslavia – Vojvodina or Croatia. They were only
deported recently, so we cannot find out anything definite
about the fate of our relatives who were sent to Poland in
1941 and 1942. There seem to be no witnesses to the

atrocities of 1941 who are still alive.

The new arrivals are accommodated in tents. They lie on a thin layer of straw – or, more accurately, on the damp ground itself. They look terrible – sick, ashen, covered in suppurating sores. We are not able to get close to them or speak to them. In the evenings, under the pretext of going to the latrine, we listen to the muffled sound that rises in the darkness like a black cloud from the other side of the barbed wire, a sound of moaning and lamenting, mixed with the crying of children. It is impossible to pick out any words. To listen to the groans and whimpers of these dying wretches is a shattering and terrifying experience.

There is a strict inspection of the huts every day. This is carried out by a young SS girl – 'the grey mouse', we call her – looking elegant and saucy in her snugly fitting uniform and her smart, shining jack-boots. Noisily and officiously she marches into the hut, accompanied by a soldier and the senior Jewish prisoner. Making theatrical, provocative gestures, the 'grey mouse' struts about, frightening us with angry cries at the sight of a bowl that is not properly washed up or a bed that has not been made tidily enough. Her speciality is to suddenly give somebody a hard clip round the ear without taking off her glove. Every day she punishes at least seven or eight prisoners in every hut for some triviality by stopping their food or withholding their bread ration. Her sole aim is to intimidate, persecute and humiliate us. This is the only reason she comes, since the Germans do not make any serious effort to get rid of the filth or curb the spread of infection, and they never will. Indeed, these are integral parts of the degrading conditions to which they subject us and in which we are left to 'live' or to die off one by one. The so-called inspections are mere formalities. Not a single one among us takes the slightest notice of this extraordinary female, with her showy antics and her perverse threats. Yet it is disgusting to have to witness these degrading scenes every morning, feel the pervading air of restlessness and watch the expression of servility on so many faces.

As a result of the extreme cold of the last few days and the compulsory fasting that has been undermining our constitutions for months, we all feel extremely weak. This terrible hunger – empty stomachs, our thoughts permanently dominated by an insane desire to eat our fill, endless talk of food. If anyone is fortunate enough to find or steal a raw turnip, it provides a feast for the whole company.

Belsen 8 November 44 I would dearly love to feel something attractive, an artistic experience, and arouse noble sentiments and tender emotions in myself. It is difficult. I try to force my imagination but I fail. There is something cruel and bestial about our existence. All human values have been reduced to nought. Bonds of friendship only survive out of habit, and what usually prevails is intolerance. Memories of past beauties have become blurred, and in our present state we are incapable of recalling earlier artistic pleasures. The brain is paralysed, the spirit crushed.

The injuries inflicted on the spirit go so deep that it is as though one's whole being were dead, as though one were shut off from the normal world of the past by a massive, solid wall. We have lost our capacity for feeling and cannot even recall our own past. It needed an immense effort for me to remember anything of my earlier life. The memories refuse to come back. We have not died, but we are dead to the world. Not only have the Nazis succeeded in destroying our right to a life in the present – and also, for many of us, a life in the future – but their sadism has also had the tragic effect of obliterating all trace of our earlier lives, all the emotions of a normal person with a normal past, even the consciousness of having once lived a life that deserved to be called human.

I try to cast my mind back – and absolutely nothing comes to me. It is as though the whole business did not concern me at all. My mind is a complete blank. In the first few weeks I had at least retained the link with my earlier life, the joy of memories and dreams. But the humiliating and degrading life in this camp has destroyed everything so brutally that to try and get away, even for a moment, from the depressing reality that surrounds us is like a pointless act of torture, something almost grotesque. My spirit is encased in a shell: nothing can soften it, nothing melt it. And to imagine this is only the fifth month, in a camp which, if one is to believe the Germans, is not even one of the worst. . . . I shall keep firmly in my mind everything that I have seen, everything that I have experienced and learnt, everything that human nature has revealed to me. It has etched itself into my soul. And I feel that in normal life (what is 'normal' – this endless suffering here or all that came before it and all that will come after it?) I shall never be able to forget the things I have discovered and the judgements I have made. I shall judge each man according to the way he has behaved, or could have behaved, in these conditions that surround us. My opinion of him, whether I respect him or not, or have an affection for him or not, will depend on how he reacted, or would have reacted, physically, psychologically and morally, to the strain of these terrible years – the strength of character he displayed, how much tension his nerves could bear. . . . Never again shall I be able to separate the world of my thoughts from the events of the war – the two are for ever inseparably linked.

Belsen 18 November 1944 My work with the children goes on in spite of everything. The others, the so-called 'adults' and 'experts', only make things difficult for me instead of helping me. Avidly I seize the slightest opportunity to get the children together so as to keep alive both in them and in myself a modicum of mental awareness and of feeling for human dignity.

We have decided to use Saturdays in the whole camp for special children's festivals, mostly of a religious character. In our particular hut we arrange programmes for the children's entertainment which are generally in keeping with our people's mentality – items like recitations, chants, choruses and little plays. Since there is a complete absence of books, I put the material together from what the children and I can call to mind, and then write it down – though we usually have to improvise the words and the verses to a large extent. By concentrating hard, my pupils succeed in remembering a lot of well-known tunes but the words are beyond our grasp, as though hidden in the depths of a cave. Then we set to work to put lines together, invent rhymes and make up poems that remind us of our beloved homeland, our proud and glorious homeland far away.

This activity comes spontaneously to me, almost instinctively, as the expression of an irresistible urge from the depths of my soul – in those rare moments when I succeed in waking my soul from its slumber. And I feel it is an urge that springs from the souls of the children themselves, for they follow my lead in their excitement, they show their desire to live, to play, a desire stronger than they are themselves. It moves me to the core.

Belsen 20 November 1944 There is something strange, something frightening in man's capacity to adapt himself to everything – the humiliation, the cruel starvation, the cramped living conditions, the foul air, the infections, the communal washplace. Conditions in this washplace are beyond what any normal person can imagine. We all stand there together, naked. Instead of doors and windows the room has gaping holes in the walls, and the wind howls in from all sides. Standing in a mass of filth, refuse and excrement, we rub ourselves down with cold water. We get used to it, just as we do to the way we are increasingly terrorised, to the callous brutality, to the air-raid alarms and the intimidation, to the rampant infections – and to the certainty of a thousand communal, lingering deaths. Incredible – people get used to it all. Slowly they sink deeper and deeper, and when their strength finally gives out, they die. It is the only answer. Those of us who are left try to hang on, slowly being dragged down like the others. O the horror of this slow death, this living death. . . .

Belsen 22 November 1944 Ch. has just died, without warning. He was a robust man, well built, sixty-five years old. Even here, in the camp, he had managed to preserve something of his wonderful vigour. Then, crushed under the burden of his misery, he did not get up for three days, lay prostrate on his bed, exhausted, starving – and died. It was all over in three days.

Yesterday roll-call lasted the entire day and far into the night, in wind and rain. Five were missing. They were 'discovered' this morning. . . .

For more than a month our meal has been reduced to one bowl of soup a day. Soup? Just a word for it – turnips boiled in water. And what water! Nothing else. Turnips in water – on the ground, in front of the barbed wire and beyond it, whatever direction we look, wherever we turn, nothing but turnips, huge mountains of turnips – turnips in the carts, turnips in front of the big gates and the galleys, turnips in the underground store rooms, turnips everywhere. . . .

The Nazis have made us crave for these turnips – these grey things usually fed to cattle – so that we are not utterly consumed by the gnawing pangs of hunger. This hunger! The whole winter long we shall have to eat these turnips – unless we die first. O blessed Germany, land of the turnip, of *Ersatz*, of concentration camps, of slavery and terrorism!

Allied aircraft are continually overhead. There is one air-raid warning after another. The whole of Germany is being bombed. Most nights there is a complete black-out: we are not allowed to light a single candle. Most of our miserable lives we spend in complete darkness. If someone happens to strike a light, however small, there is a great outcry, and everybody starts to shout and curse. We are in fear and trembling of the Germans, who have become even more savage. Whenever they see the slightest flicker of a light, they shoot. In the Dutch hut they have already killed a man and a woman.

Those who are 'fortunate' enough to work outside with the Germans have brought us the good news that Germany has almost reached the end of the road. The civilian population are subjected to endless bombing and are in desperate straits. The end is near. But the officers and soldiers have not changed – they are just as arrogant, just as brutal, just as cruel. We have heard that the whole of the Balkans has been liberated. The same report says that a Balkan Federation has been founded, with Salonica as its capital. There are other incredible reports too. Even if some of the details are not accurate, the news of this development as a whole is true enough – and that is what matters.

I am trying to imagine what the liberation of my country will be like, and the immense happiness that will fill the new society. The thought of it almost turns my head. Sitting here in the midst of this misery and letting such visions pass through my mind, I feel as though my nerves will snap under the strain of such unbelievable happiness. Then, when this tension has passed, I envisage a flood of emotion welling up, like the eruption of a volcano, and the tears that have for so long been fought back will pour forth. Such happiness would be too great, too much for us to bear, would cause us too much pain.

But no – we shall find the strength to stand up to this strain, and after a while everything will become clear and find its true form. The nightmare will pass and give way to emotions that are honest and pure, and beauty will again become something natural. That time *will* come, *must* come, whoever is there to receive it. This is what matters.

II

Belsen December 1944 I thought the end had come and there was nothing more for me to record. But there *is* no end. One day follows another – fearful, terrifying dark days. If only we could see the end, whatever it is. . . .

We are all exhausted, reduced to a shadow. The food they

give us gets less day by day. It is three days since we saw a
crust of bread. A few prisoners have saved some tiny pieces
and have now spread them out – only to find that they have
gone mouldy. Bread is like gold here. Anything can be had
for bread, and people will risk everything to get some.
Stealing is on the increase, especially at night. Someone
suggested we should take turns to keep watch to catch the
pilferers. We did it for two nights, in pitch darkness, with a
lot of noise and in an atmosphere of tension. No one slept.
But it produced nothing.

Those who still have a little bread keep it under their
pillows – or rather, they make it into a pillow, so that it is
safer while they are asleep. It is especially the mothers who
do this, in order to make sure that their children have
something to nibble. Those in the labour gangs, who are
out at work all day, have to carry all their food with them in
a bag the whole time. 'All their food' means six days' ration
at the most, that is, half a loaf. Sooner or later they all
succumb to the temptation of eating the whole six days'
ration in a single day.

As we were going to work yesterday – the women's
labour gang, that is – we saw some potatoes lying on the
road. Either they must have dropped off a lorry or been
thrown away on their long and arduous march by some of
the last batch of prisoners who had decided on their long
march that they would rather die of starvation than of
exhaustion. We know that feeling. Our hungry eyes lighted
on the potatoes, and a woman bent down to pick one up.
But in the same instant she was frightened into dropping it
again by the savage shouts of the soldier in charge of us,
who could not tolerate the thought of such gluttony. . . .

For over six weeks the Germans have stopped all the jobs

we used to do inside the camp. Everybody has to work outside in one or other of the labour gangs. No one is spared: children over fourteeen, old men – they are all sent out on forced labour. Nobody is made to see that the huts are kept clean and tidy – that does not interest the Germans any more. No more school classes, no more cleaning parties – everything is in a state of confusion, a mass of decay and filth.

In order to make as many prisoners available for work as possible, the Germans are redoubling their terror tactics. We are made to get up every morning at four o'clock, before dawn. We feel like hunted animals being chased hither and thither in a state of fear and terror. It is mid-winter, freezing cold. By five we have to be assembled on the parade ground in proper order. It is the first roll-call of the day, when we report for work. It is still dark, and we wait for the duty officer to count us and send us out to work. Frozen to the marrow, starving, weakened by months of suffering, we feel our strength ebbing away. But we are forbidden to leave the parade ground, or even to move. Many faint and collapse under the cold and the malnutrition. Twice I began to feel dizzy myself and almost fell down. The ground acquires a mystical power of attraction in such moments. How dearly I would have loved to lie down and rest! But I managed to summon up all my strength. It is no joke to become ill in this place. There is nobody in the world to help you if you do. You just peg out, that's all.

It is seven or half-past before the German condescends to turn up to count us. He starts by showering abuse on all of us, kicking people at random for some trivial reason or other. Then he picks out his victims, those who dare to try and explain why they cannot work, and sets about 'converting' them. Grabbing hold of them, he punches them and hits them in the stomach, knocks them down and drags them along the ground, kicking them the whole time. Then he forces them to stand up and get back into line. . . .

Belsen December 1944 The camp commandant has been replaced by one Kramer, a former commandant from the camp at Auschwitz. That speaks for itself. The camp routine is getting harsher day by day. The Germans make regular swoops on the huts. Instead of punishing individual prisoners by stopping their meal or their bread ration, they have introduced new measures for the whole camp as a general punishment. Who cares that there are sick people and young children in the camp?

We are gripped by the sickening feeling that from now on nobody will care what happens to us. We are totally at the mercy of the new commandant, this rabid, anti-Semitic monster. He is absolute master of the camp and answerable to no one. There is nobody beyond him to whom we can appeal – even God is powerless.

Kramer does as he wishes. Fresh loads of prisoners roll in ceaselessly. Between the compounds and the barbed wire fences endless columns of pitiful, strange-looking creatures move around – terrible they look, ghosts, not like human beings at all. We stare across at them, and they fix us with a terrifying gaze. To them we probably look the same.

There is not enough room for all of us. Every day we have to move somewhere else, and conditions are becoming more and more cramped. Finally they order us to sleep two to a bunk, so that the three tiers together now hold six persons. In this way we have made half our hut available for some of the new arrivals.

We now notice the mud, rain and damp inside the huts as well, which are very badly built and now in a poor state, full of holes. But there is nothing we can do about it: we just have to stay here. We are engulfed in our own stinking sea of germs, lice and fleas, and everything around us is putrid and slimy. As we are literally lying on top of each other, we provide a perfect breeding-ground for the lice. It is imposs-ible to catch them and kill them all – a hopeless task. The bunks are so narrow that we cannot move, and to find room to sit down or rest is out of the question. This infernal confinement! Think of Hut 25, where the French and Hun-garian women are kept, together with others, all shut up in one heap. They are being driven insane. It is like a den of thieves, the Frenchwomen say. Have we reached the depths of our suffering yet? Or is there worse to come?

Belsen, December 1944 Kramer has done away with the position of senior Jewish prisoner. The Jews no longer have any say in the running of the huts, and the committee of senior prisoners has been disbanded. The members of this committee were in fact all corrupt and unscrupulous. They behaved with utter callousness towards the general mass of prisoners and did nothing but pilfer ruthlessly from the others, use their privileged position for their own personal advantage and curry favour with the Germans by forcing thousands of their fellows to work for their captors. Their conduct was disgraceful in every respect. I have already written about them – it is a subject on its own. . . .

What matters to us at the moment is Kramer and his gang. He has put a new detachment in charge of us, all 'Aryans' – German, Polish and French convicts. They are well-fed young men, with the strength of bulls. They strut

to and fro, hitting out at us as they please. They wear
convict dress – striped trousers and long shirts with a big
number on the back. But the most terrible thing about them
is that they have the mentality of criminals of the worst
kind. They are true creatures of the devil – the devil Kramer
– and are no longer human. Cold, cruel, sadistic – had I not
seen with my own eyes the obscene delight they take in
beating us, I would never have thought it possible. The
Germans have made them what they are, have turned them
into wild animals in human shape, and it is as though this
makes them want to avenge themselves on us.

These hardened criminals are now our masters, free to do
what they like with us and our children. Common slaves
themselves, they hold us enslaved in their power. The devil
has fettered us together. The bestial Nazis always think of
something new when it comes to finding ways of degrading
people and 'finishing them off.' The new commandant and
the new *Kapos* vent their fury chiefly on the men, persecuting them mercilessly. One place where our men are made to
work is the 'tree-stump party'. They are worked to death
here, hacking out the roots of trees. When they get back in
the evening, not one of them is in a normal condition – they
are beaten black and blue, their faces and bodies swollen and
covered in blood. Yesterday, December 30, two were club-
bed to death. The same day two more were carried back to
the camp on stretchers by their comrades. The *Kapos* beat
the women as well, or, even worse, force them to become
prostitutes.

Belsen January 1945 The new regime is like a nightmare. The
Kapos behave like bloodthirsty beasts, insane in their rage
and their obscenity. We hear no news, nothing that could

restore us to life. Deathly silence: we have all been stricken dumb by the ghastly terror. And no end in sight.

Belsen January 1945 I have managed to speak to a few of the women transported here from Auschwitz. Most of them are Jews from Poland, Greece and Hungary. They told us what they had gone through in Auschwitz. In the time they were there, from 1943 to 1944, hundreds of thousands had been wiped out, while they themselves were among the few who had miraculously survived. 'Words cannot describe what we have been though,' they said. They tell us of the mass murders, of the 99 per cent who have been massacred in the gas chambers, of the obscenities to which they were subjected. And as they talk about these things, their eyes seem to be asking, silently, whether we believe them: sometimes, they say, they themselves even begin to doubt whether they are speaking the truth. They fear nobody will believe them and will put their stories down as the tales of lunatics. Of all the women sent to Auschwitz, only a few hundred have survived. The men and the children were gassed at the very beginning, together with the elderly and the weak. A Jewish woman from Greece told me that only 300 women were still alive out of the 70,000 Greek Jews who had been interned with her in Auschwitz, and that she herself had been made to watch her parents and her whole family burn to death.

Remarkably enough, these women, fugitives from hell, who had worked in the kitchens, in the stores and – believe it or not – in the orchestra, all look healthy and comparatively well. It is strange to compare their physical condition with ours. But they told us that in Auschwitz the prisoners had had sufficient to eat, and that by helping each other, they had managed to get all they needed. In general, they said, they had not gone hungry but the fear of death hung over all of them: each one saw himself the victim of a remorseless, irreversible fate, waiting to be swallowed up by the flames of the inferno.

The death factory, the women told us, worked at full stretch every day. Row upon row of men and women, sometimes hundreds, sometimes one or two thousand, stood in line every day outside the big shower room until it was their turn to be gassed. The smoke poured out of the crematorium, and as they watched, they knew what it meant. It told them that there was the furnace where the bodies of their relatives had been burnt and where their own lives too would soon end.

But in their camp, said our fellow-sufferers from Auschwitz – who were astonished to hear about the systematic starvation to which we were subjected – no one went hungry. The end is the same – only the means are different. In Auschwitz it is a quick, ruthless procedure, mass murder in the gas chambers; in Belsen it is a sadistic, long-drawn-out process of starvation, of violence, of terror, of the deliberate spreading of infection and disease.

Belsen January 1945 For a long while now they have stopped taking us to the central washroom, where we were able to have a hot shower – while the soldiers detailed to guard us insolently looked on and mocked us. In spite of our embarrassment we somehow felt happy that we were clean for a few days. But now – nothing, neither shower not hot water. All that is now just a dream. All we have left is the washroom, which is frozen up and full of infection. We all undress there together, hastily, knocking into each other the whole time. There is no sense in waiting our turn – there are too many of us, all crowding round the taps. We only hope the water will not be cut off. . . . In the freezing cold we hurriedly take off our clothes and wash ourselves, men and women together, without embarrassment and without paying the slightest heed to the others. Sex has no meaning here. The main thing is to scrape some of the dirt off. Our teeth chatter, and the icy water burns our skin. It hurts – but who cares. . . .

Our bodies have adapted themselves to the hunger. Sometimes a man may feel so wracked with hunger that he can no longer stand it and devours his entire supply of bread – three or four days' ration – in one go. At other times people exchange the greater part of their clothes for one or two rations of soup which the pilferers offer them. After bolting down such unaccustomed quantities of foul food, they are overcome by nausea and feel worse than ever. Their digestion cannot cope with the food; they throw up, and are as hungry as before.

Meals are coming more and more irregularly. The soup meant for midday does not arrive until five or six, and supper, which consists of a few drops of boiled water or a tiny piece of processed cheese, has been cut out altogether and arrives either the following morning or not at all. So sometimes sixteen or twenty hours can elapse without a thing to eat. When the food does arrive, the starving prisoners make a rush for the soup pots, and a few hours later comes the inevitable consequence – the whole place reeks of diarrhoea.

Belsen January 1945 The whole camp is now infected with lice and other vermin, and dysentery has spread alarmingly.

It is caused by a general infection of the intestines and spreads rapidly. There is no way of checking it and no cure. It literally eats the body away.

There is muck and disease everywhere – on the wooden floor of the huts, in the bunks, the washrooms, the yard and the latrines (open holes for men and women together). It penetrates everywhere.

Although we are all weak from enteric fever and on the brink of starvation, we do our best to keep the place as clean as possible – a pathetic and pointless activity. We are desperate, almost out of our minds, a mass of starving, exhausted bodies, half dead, looking like skeletons, with excrement everywhere.

Belsen January 1945 General malnutrition. It is as much as we can do to move. Nobody is able to walk upright, in a normal way; they all drag themselves along, swaying from side to side. Whole families die in the space of a few days. Old mother M. died quickly; two days later it was her husband's turn, then the children's, victims of malnutrition and the lice. One of the children was a short-sighted young lad who could not cope with the lice crawling over his body. They had penetrated his skin and even got into his eyelashes, and his chest was black with thousands of them. We have never seen anything like it, and no one could have imagined such a sight. They have eaten him away, body and mind, making him look like a mental defective. He used to be a very intelligent boy, they said, Today he slowly drags his skinny, flea-ridden body from one end of the hut to the other, moaning and whimpering. The others avoid him, and his sister and his brother are afraid to go near him. A few days ago he spent the entire night struggling pathetically from one bunk to the next, begging to be given a little room, but they all pushed him away in disgust. We all lie two to a bunk, but no one would share with him and there was no spare bunk. So, with no place to lay his wretched body, he just died. A tragic story – but far from unique. There are thousands of such cases in this camp, especially among the old prisoners. Theirs is a terrible fate. They are just waiting for their pitiful, horrible end to come, an agonising, lingering death as their bodies moulder and decay.

Belsen January 1945 Death has now finally settled among us, our most faithful companion, every present. As a result of their brutal treatment poeple are dying in masses from malnutrition, from beatings, from dysentery, from the bugs. They simply collapse and fall down – more and more of them. Many of my friends have already come to the end of their days. One, two, three, four – and then one begins to mistake the dead for the living. Not that there is much difference. We are skeletons that can still move, whereas they are skeletons that cannot. But there is a third category – those who lie stretched out on their bunks, still breathing slightly but unable to move. It is just a question of waiting for them to die and make room for others. Small wonder that when we count our numbers, we confuse them with the dead.

Our worst experience is when we are made to move into other huts. We have had to do so two or three times a month recently. All the things that go to make up our tragic situation – our rotting bodies, our rags and bits of cloth, our bulky, useless parcels, the cries of the sick, who are too numerous for us to help them all, the groans of the dying who have been left outside and abandoned to the quarrelling, cursing and wailing going on in the midst of all the confusion – all this is suddenly taken out of the reeking suffocation of the huts and dumped in a heap in the mud and rain outside. To see everything in its naked reality in the light of a cold, grey sky makes it look even more pathetic and more pitiful. These moves from one hut to another generally produce a few more dead than usual. For those of us who are fitter than the rest, these transfers are sheer agony; for the sick and the elderly they mean certain death.

Belsen February 1945 Typhoid fever has begun to dominate the scene. The diagnosis is said to be very involved. At the moment it is chiefly the children who are affected, but they can also die from other causes, and we do not know which. One fine day, as the expression has it, two little girls died in a bed close by, quietly, one after the other. Their mother, a simple, very attractive woman, watched over them as a wolf guards her cubs. When she realised they were dead, she burst into piercing shrieks of agony. Then she began to chant dirges, making up the words with incredible skill as she went along and whispering gently to the tiny bodies. But now she shuffles about with her hair unkempt, does not bother to take off her rags, totally neglects herself and has a glint of madness in her eyes. Life has lost all meaning for her.

Belsen February 1945 Two successive nights I was on duty in the old people's hut. Since almost all of them are sick, they do not get up. They were horrible nights. For one thing all the work has to be done in complete darkness because of the air-raid alarms. All one can do is to comfort them, bring them their chamber-pots, then empty the pots in the nearby latrines. The foul smell is everywhere.

The sick die a slow death as they lie there, rotting away while still alive – I can think of no other way of putting it. Yet they still have an unbelievable craving to live, incessantly wailing and crying out for help. They often irritate me. Most of them are women from the prosperous middle classes in western European countries like Holland, Belgium and France, who used to live comfortable and protected lives. They are quite incapable of grasping the reality of their present situation, and in consequence behave very badly. At the same time they look so miserable.

Threading my way between the narrow rows of bunks, I pull off their useless, foul-smelling rags, the remnants of their one-time prosperity, and do what I can to keep their beds clean and help them wash their faces. They are a terrible sight, these living corpses, these pallid, ghostly faces, contorted with pain. And everything in complete darkness.

I am haunted by a sense of fear and misery. During the first night three of the sick died, and I had to lay out the corpses and cover them over. Dead bodies are so heavy, and I have scarcely any strength left. But otherwise I was not afraid of them – they were lying everywhere: one simply 'lives' with them and thus becomes indifferent to it all.

In the course of the second night I had a real struggle with Frau P., who went out of her mind. I had to prevent her from scaring the others by jumping up and clinging on to them in the darkness, as was her habit. Three times she jumped out of bed, and each time I held her back. It was far from easy. She had her own way of wailing and imploring – it was terrible. Apart from her insane outbursts, she seems far from being a stupid woman – she is desperately unhappy, that's all. She is said to have been very intelligent but to have gradually become insane as a result of a series of 'unexpected' tragedies that struck her in the war, so that now she was completely mad. She kept on trying to explain something or other to me, striving with all her might to convince me but without losing her temper. There was despair in every word she spoke as she pleaded with me. On the other hand there are three really hysterical women here, who make the rest of us feel frightened. The two nights I spent in this madhouse have shattered my nerves. I suddenly feel ten years older. So terrible was the experience that it took me days to recover.

Belsen February 1945 The corruption that has long been rampant throughout the camp has become even worse since the convicts were put in charge of us. It is only what one would expect. When they took over from the Jews, the worst pilferers withdrew from the scene and kept quiet, together with those who had ruled the roost for the past few months. But this only lasted a short while. Sizing up the situation, they quickly realised that it would soon develop to their advantage, even more so than previously. So in these ideal conditions they went to work, greedily stealing anything they could lay their hands on and persecuting the others. They quickly came to an agreement with our new masters, the convicts, and eagerly joined them in a barter system in which they offered to help in the *Kapos'* savage attacks on the prisoners. All this is going on in our hut, before our very eyes, and in the other huts it is the same. Traitors, criminals – they deserve to be hanged.

They are perpetually chewing, and insolently stuff themselves with the choicest delicacies while the mass of the prisoners, starving and half-dead, stare at them with lifeless eyes. What monsters, what scum. Their luck has gone to their heads and they are beside themselves with glee, shouting abuse at everybody, afraid of no one, prepared for anything. They beat us mercilessly and threaten us if anyone dares to talk of reporting them to the *Kapos*, and take quick vengeance by delivering any 'uncooperative' elements into the hands of the *Kapos* when the labour gangs are sent out in the morning. Thanks to these despicable wretches, the *Kapos* always manage to find fresh victims for their infamous so-called 'death gangs.'

No words can describe the brutality of these treacherous, repulsive cratures, these murderers' lackeys, these ruthless, blood-stained villains. Each one thinks only of himself; none has any feeling for his fellows. Many of the women have sold themselves. Without a moment's thought quite young girls, who know nothing of life and its principles, have seized the opportunity that the tragic situation offered them. Gorging and drinking-parties, dancing, laughing, flirting, pretty clothes, silk stockings – this is the sort of life they lead in the society of the *Kapos*.

The hunger presses upon our minds. I feel my strength ebbing away – mental as well as physical strength. Things slip out of my mind: I cannot take events in properly, cannot think straight, cannot grasp the full horror of the situation. Only occasionally does a moment of comprehension flash through my mind, and I ask myself what sinister, malicious, perverse force it can be that can plunge a whole civilisation into such a monstrous, perverse situation.

Belsen February 1945 I am sharing my bunk with Frau G., a

rather stout woman of about fifty, who has become virtually paralysed through various ailments, hunger and
nicotine. She never gets up: as heavy as lead, oblivious to
feeling, she is as though strapped to the bed. The whole day
I try to find a place to put my body, some corner of this
squalid bunk where I can rest my dying limbs for a while. It
has become almost impossible to breathe. . . .

In the evenings I come back to this damp hole on the
bottom tier of the bed, with three adults and two children
lying on the two bunks above me. Our bed stands against
the worm-eaten boards which serve as a wall, with the rain
running down it the whole time. The window and the door
are also close by. The damp has penetrated everything – our
clothes, our blankets, our bodies and everything else in the
hut is wet through, literally soaking. Water and mire are
everywhere, inside and out. The air has the suffocating
smell of typhoid fever and reeks of the urine that trickles
through the hut the whole time. A bed? It bears no resemb-
lance to a bed. It is a mass of sodden mud.

Every morning when I wake up and get out of this hole
my face is swollen and my eyes are stuck together; it takes
me two hours to open them properly and see where I am. I
wonder each time whether I am going blind. This is not a
bed but a grave, a grave for two.

Belsen February 1945 On the twelfth of this month it will be a
year since we were arrested in Cetinje. For much of this
time we have cherished vain hopes and crazy illusions. At
the beginning we felt almost happy, despite being prisoners, for we were almost certain that all would soon be over –
a total misconception, for the war was in full swing at the
time. Since then we have become very sceptical, and these

terrible, long winter nights, beset with fear and hunger, with vermin and death, give us no ray of hope.

The hunger, the hunger – is there anything on earth more terrible, more soul-destroying for a man? I am haunted by the sight of these suffering faces, the faces of despairing, suffering animals thronging round some stinking pot of stagnant, lukewarm water they call our soup. That is what we now get as soup – just water, with a few pieces of putrid turnip boiled in it, often two whole days before it is doled out. They fill the pots at once, put the lids on – 'to keep the soup warm', they say – and only take them off a day or two days later when it is ladled out. So it soon goes bad – but we have had our food. . . .

There was a time when we enjoyed the turnips, boiled or raw. We were ravenous then – now we are hungrier than ever. Our bodies are ravaged by hunger; we drag ourselves about like limp, wet rags, while others simply collapse from malnutrition and give up the ghost. Yet no one touches this soup. No one is capable of eating it. Immediately after each meal it is poured on to the garbage heap, which grows bigger and bigger each day and gives off an acrid stench.

Strange and wonderful bits of news still reach our ears from time to time, but now they do not seem to be meant for us any more: they are like rumours from another world, a world beyond the grave, beyond our own graves.

All we know or see is the slow plod of endless columns of miserable figures filing past, thousands and thousands of prisoners from all the camps that the Germans have had to evacuate. It is clear that the Germans are in retreat and are dragging their victims with them. This is where they are assembling them. But there is a rumour that we are going to be taken away from here as well: the Allies are said to be close by, so that the Germans would have to evacuate the whole area and send us somewhere else. Rumours like these, the air of uncertainty, with the possibility that we may all in the end be wiped out – the fact that Kramer is here makes this all the more likely – is a form of mental torture that has driven us more than once to the brink of madness.

And the whole time row upon row of pitiful figures, walking skeletons, shuffle past along the road. From the other side of the barbed wire we watch them file by and wonder who they are. What is going to happen to them – or to us? How will they end up – or we end up? What shall we be made to do? What are they waiting for? And the English – what do they intend to do? What plans are they thinking up? They have the situation in their control – are they going to use us all in order to preserve the position that suits them best? They could have finished Germany off long ago. What do they care about human life, about the sufferings of the oppressed, about their death and their rotting corpses? Nothing. Freedom? A confidence trick, which they play as long as it suits them. They exploit smaller countries, abusing their privileged position in the hierarchy of nations. That's why the situation is as it is. The only thing that counts is the policy of the Soviet Union and faith in the triumph of the new society. Otherwise what meaning can it all have? Is war rooted in human nature? If there is no real victory, and the whole world does not become socialist, what is the point of our life? So that we can start all over again, with fresh massacres and new depravities? I am beginning to despair of humankind.

We wish for so many things, have an avid desire for everything. Are we really approaching our end? What about the Jewish question? Where and how is this diabolical

comedy going to finish? And our Jewish homeland –
where? – why? – how? – in what form? Perhaps our agony
will never end. I have never before been so tormented by
such thoughts, never asked myself such questions. And
now, at this moment, I feel that the problem will go on for
ever, like a wound that never heals. Our precious Slav
homeland, the land we love – will you still want us? Shall
we have become strangers to you too? Or have I gone mad
to ask such ridiculous qestions!

Belsen March 1945 Everything we see around us, everything
we see going on, makes us begin to doubt whether we are
still human beings – indeed, to doubt the humanity of man.
We are starting to put strange questions to ourselves. Yesterday I had a long talk with Professor K. He is in the sick
bay, utterly exhausted, his face and limbs terribly swollen
from frost-bite and boils, his body covered in running
sores. In addition he is suffering from dysentery and all
manner of other disorders. I visit him regularly so as to help
relieve his suffering to some extent. We talk about the
tragedy that has befallen us and ask in our incredulity
whether there can be such a thing as normal life again after
all we have lived through here. It is scarcely conceivable.
This seems to be the end of our journey, the terrible, despicable final act of our existence.

We analysed the attitudes of various people. Everybody
helps himself as best he can, and the question arises whether
we are all just being subjected to this severe test in order to
discover how much 'moral sense of direction' or 'power of
survival' the one or other of us has. Is that what it is – power
of survival, the struggle against death, the urge to self-
preservation? Is that where the measure of a man's strength

and life-force resides? Must man become a savage, a wild animal, in order to stay alive?

Would that then mean that the rest of us, who are not able to fight our way through like this and resort to such brutality, are unfit to survive and doomed to destruction? My mind is just a blank. Is that the highest law of nature, the law of all living creatures? Yes, some might say. Well and good. But what then? What about the power of human reason – does that count for nothing? The human mind has created many ethical laws and concepts that conflict with the laws dictated by animal instinct. What has happened to these laws and concepts? Have they no relevance here?

Indeed they have, and I am firmly convinced that those for whom ethical principles are fundamental laws, and to whom such laws have become second nature – a kind of human instinct taking the place of animal instinct – will not go under. Such men are not doomed to perish in the brutal struggle that rages around them. And I am certain that I too shall succeed in coming to grips with my situation, in sticking to my principles and helping to preserve humane values – always provided that my health stays as it is. For everything does indeed depend on one's health, on one's physical powers of resistance. This is the most important thing, and on it rests my ability to retain a sense of integrity and honour. In other words, it is not a personal achievement of my own. I cannot see my way out of the situation. . . .

We continued our discussion. Who is right and who is wrong? What attitude should one adopt? We examined the possibilities. There is the moral standpoint of J., the ideas of L., the pragmatism of Li., the logical approach of R., and the willingness of K. and his family to compromise – which led us to touch on the subject of 'the art of giving', the question of how one man assumes the right to dispense charity and another to receive it. We also thought it appropriate to look into I.'s quite extraordinary ability as a business man, an ability that takes on a particularly objectionable quality in conditions like ours.

In Professor K.'s view, morality, as we understand the term, does not apply in concentration camps and is out of place there, even unnecessary, and we must needs dispense with it if we really intend to survive and help to build the new world in which it will prevail. Mind, he maintained, is subject to matter, is merely the sublimation of matter, its 'intellectual superstructure', as Marx called it. Consequently it is natural and inevitable that matter will reject mind when mind is irrelevant and has become an anomaly.

Yet somehow this does not convince me. And in the specific cases we were discussing, what does it mean to talk of the victory of matter? It means simply to compromise with the enemy, to betray one's principles, to deny spiritual values in the interests of saving one's skin. Applying the argument to our own situation, it would mean turning oneself into a prostitute, or currying favour with the Nazi hangmen, or shrinking like a coward from the sight of so much misery, so much slaughter, eating what one has stolen from others and dancing round the piles of corpses with the murderers. It means sacrificing one's reason and one's honour and bartering away one's principles – in the last analysis, therefore, it means saving oneself at the expense of others. But is human life ultimately so precious that we can permit all these atrocities in order to preserve it?

Belsen March 1945 We have all been smitten with a fever akin to typhoid and have to stay in bed. A special barbed wire fence has been erected round our hut, and we have been put in quarantine. I ran a fever for a fortnight, starting with a temperature of 40° and 41°, then 38° and 39°. There are no drugs. Those who can, stick it out. Throughout these two weeks I had terrible headaches and constantly felt like throwing up. My hunger completely disappeared. I became delirious. The only feeling I had was that I was very near to death – not just that death was close at hand in a general sense but this time very close to me personally. I felt its breath upon me. I died slowly, fully conscious. My body had no sensation at all but just seemed to gradually cease functioning. The only thought left in my mind was of death.

Those lying around me were also in the throes of death, dying one after the other. I now have the middle bunk. Below me is Frau K. In the course of a single month she lost her husband and her daughter. Silent, racked with pain, her face turned away, she lies there stretched out, waiting for her turn to come. She groans incessantly, although I am sure she cannot really feel pain any more: She just cannot go on and has stopped wanting to live. It is her life, her miserable existence that is the cause of her suffering, and she is impatient for it to be over, that's all.

On the bunk above me is C., totally apathetic, who spends his whole time trying to convince the others that he is neither sick nor insane, neither foul-smelling nor ridden with disease. To the right of me two old men have died, F. and K. Half-asleep, half-awake, I shared F.'s agony the whole night through; the next night I listened as K. gave out his last feeble coughs. It is all so simple. First one stops breathing, then the next. No one can help anyone else, and the corpses just lie there in the bunks beside those who are still alive or only half-dead. The living and the dead side by side – though there is barely any distinction between the two.

Death has become an everyday event and leaves us completely indifferent. We have given up thinking about being rescued and have stopped counting the days as we used to. There is no point in knowing when the Allies will arrive, though it seems certain that they are only a few dozen kilometres away. For the present our closest and most loyal ally is death. And if we do begin to count the days again, then it is not with an eye to the moment of our liberation but in order to see how long the one or the other of us can still survive. There is a kind of medical curiosity in us, a strange obsession. There was a time when I was convinced I would only live another month or two. Now, having somehow miraculously got over the bout of typhoid fever, which taxed my power of endurance to the limit, I give myself only ten or fifteen days at the most.

This brief semi–existence that is left to me I spend in the company of other ghosts, some living, some dead. The corpses are still here, lying in our beds. There is no one to take them away and nowhere to put them in the crowded hut. In the yard outside they lie piled on top of each other in great heaps that grow higher every day. The crematorium is not capable of burning them all.

They have stopped bringing us any food from over there, except for an occasional container of rancid soup. Some pull up a few blades of grass and boil them, others rummage in the garbage pails for potato peelings. The corrupt ones among us still manage to get something but even they can no longer avoid the infection, the suffering and death. Death is everywhere, hovering above us, threatening to pounce at any moment.

No one concerns himself with us any more. The Nazis no

longer appear. We know that their end is at hand. But so is ours, and they realise that too. There is nothing left for them to do in the camp, so they don't come near us any more. As soon as they had finished the diabolical job they were **given** and were seen to have carried it out satisfactorily, they withdrew and left us to die off one by one. The *Kapos* still behave like monsters, walking around and lashing out at us at random. There are even a few among them who take pity on us – for a moment or two. I noticed it myself – but it is pure chance. In the main they still take a callous attitude towards us and sneer at our misfortune.

Belsen April 1945 I am deeply ashamed to be experiencing such things. Bodies lie rotting in the mire. Cases of canni-balism are said to have occurred in one of the blocks nearby. According to the German doctor who came to our com-pound to check on how the extermination was progressing, more than 17,000 of the total of 45,000 prisoners had died in each of the last two months, February and March – that is, some 35,000 in all.

If only it were a straightforward, humane death. . . . No, I refuse to die like this – I refuse! Better to put an end to it all as quickly as possible, like a human being. Are we supposed to let ourselves decay and perish, physically and psycholog-ically, slowly but inexorably sinking into the void of total exhaustion, smelling of suppuration and contamination, dying bit by bit like beasts? We die like animals here, not like human beings. Why wait? To do so is to trample on human dignity. What dishonour, what unspeakable dis-grace! I look around at this gloomy hut full of ghosts, of hatred and degradation, these sick, helpless creatures unable to move, these living corpses, already decaying, a black abyss into which a whole civilisation is slipping. And I resolve that as long as my brain is still capable of functioning, I shall never allow myself to suffer an end like that. It is man's duty to die like a man and avoid a fate that is worse than any death – a death that is no death. . . .

Belsen April 1945 It is horrible to see what man has turned into. The blackest moments of the Middle Ages and the Inquisition are being repeated here, only in a form a thousand times worse. Our 'civilised' and 'cultured' Germany of the twentieth century will bear the stigma of dishonour for ever. The vilest, most savage humiliation imaginable has turned life here into something that no longer bears any relationship to life as we understand it. In reality we are dealing with the barbaric annihilation of thousands of human beings – of this there can be no doubt, *not the slightest doubt.*

One needs only to observe what has been going on here to reach the inescapable conclusion that Belsen was not built as a temporary camp for civilian or military prisoners, men and women detained on political or security grounds until the end of hostilities. Nothing of the kind. Belsen was deliberately established and equipped in order to exterminate thousands of human beings methodically and with scientific thoroughness. And even if the situation lasts only for another month, it is unlikely that a single one of us will survive.

Interview between Hanna Lévy-Hass and Eike Geisel

Eike Geisel: I should like to open our conversation with a question about the circumstances in which you wrote your diary. The Nazis' main objective was to dispose of their thousands of victims without trace, leaving no survivors or physical evidence that could testify to their policy of systematic murder. When one thinks of deportation and of imprisonment in concentration camps, the question may sound almost ludicrous – but weren't you taking a great risk by writing these things down?

Hanna Lévy-Hass: It did not strike me as anything special. It was quite natural and logical. Before I was transferred to the concentration camp, I was in a Gestapo prison in Cetinje, in Montenegro, where I had been a teacher. They put us in prison there together with the last of the Jews, some thirty in all, and others from Montenegro, not only Jews. That was where I began to write. I felt it had become a sort of necessity for me to do so. It was dangerous to some extent, certainly, though I was not especially courageous, and it was not a mark of particular heroism – rather the expression of a deep spiritual need. I remember it was more dangerous in Cetinje, because that was a small prison, and we were continuously under guard. But in the concentration camp it was not so bad. The Nazis, the SS 'supermen', took good care not to get too close to the prisoners in the huts, because we were not regarded as human beings. They only came close in order to shout at us or beat us or pick people out for the slave gangs at the 'roll calls'.

You must try to understand what these roll-calls were like, though it is hard to imagine. Probably it *was* dangerous to write things down, but I didn't think about it. I had a little notebook, and when I found the time and the courage, I wrote something down. Sometimes I jotted down only a few words or a few lines and wrote them up afterwards.

There were a few people I trusted who knew I was writing something down, and they helped me to find a quiet corner. No one attached much importance to it. They knew I was writing and that I felt the need to do so. That was all. When the Germans came, it was not to check our things but when someone refused to work or something had been stolen – food, for example. Then they made a great set-out.

Learning at 'school' with the children was more risky, because it was forbidden. That's why we did it at times when the Germans were unable to come. Sometimes they came unawares, and then it was dangerous. But the children were so clever that nobody could see what we were doing. I was well aware that this was dangerous, but writing wasn't. I kept the diary in my pocket with other odds and ends, and at the time when we were to be transferred to the camp at Theresienstadt, I took it with me in a little bag.

When I got home – to Jugoslavia, that is – I did not give it much thought, but a few weeks later – it may have been months – I copied it out (Shortly after my return I had found a job with Radio Belgrade, working on the editorial staff of the French language section). I made between ten and twenty copies, and people who were interested in it, including Party members, read it. But that was all.

In 1948 or 1949, when I arrived in Israel, I was asked whether I could tell them anything about Belsen. I could, of course, and because nobody could read Serbo-Croat, I translated my diary into French, but there were only a few private copies. During the Eichmann trial in Jerusalem in 1961 I gave it to an official of the F.I.R. (International Federation of Resistance Fighters), which included it in its publications.

E.G.: I tried to explain to you earlier why we considered it necessary to publish your diary in West Germany at the present time. How do you see it?

H.L.-H.: I never actually thought of publishing it again after it had appeared over fifteen years earlier under the auspices of the F.I.R. There have been five editions in all. The first was in Jugoslavia in 1946, in Serbo-Croat – only a very few copies. Then the F.I.R. published it in French and German in 1961. A Hebrew translation was made by the Association of Israeli Resistance Fighters in 1963, and almost ten years later the left-wing *La Nuova Italia* brought it out in Italian. Finally a private edition appeared in Israel in 1974, on which your present edition is based.

As to why it did not occur to me to publish it again, I would say that it seemed inappropriate, besides which I had no personal reason for doing so. But I understand that it was important to make it available to a wide circle of German readers, since hitherto the various editions had generally been printed for those who thought as I did and had fought the same fight as I had. I have nothing new to tell these people, nor do I need to convince them. But I am sure it is important for the Germans to read it, especially when people try to make out that the past was merely a myth, and when one continually hears it said that the sort of experiences I went through are pure imagination, that these crimes never really took place and that it is all a pathological invention on the part of the Communists and the Jews. In such a situation there is room, I think, for a book that tells the truth, so I can see the point of your wishing to publish my diary in book form.

I have been reading a lot recently about Neo-Nazi incidents in Germany. Are the West Germans prepared to believe the lies that former Nazis put out? Do you know why such things are happening? People didn't want to tell the younger generation the truth about what had gone on. That is why those who deny that such things happened are able to behave as they do. If one forgets such things, or is ignorant of them, they can easily occur again. But if one wants to stop them happening again, one must know the facts. Those who cannot remember how things were must be made to live through those times again. If one knows little or nothing about the past, there is no way of preventing history from repeating itself. Left-wing activities in Germany are closely watched and left-wingers are quickly charged and put on trial. But if one follows the Maidanek trial* in Düsseldorf, for instance, one can see that anti-Nazi trials in West Germany are a farce. . . .

E.G.: There are no 'anti-Nazi' trials in West Germany. . . .

H.L.-H.: That is precisely why I maintain that we must tell the truth about what really happened and contradict all

* In the concentration camp of Maidanek, in Lublin, some 1,400 prisoners died between 1942 and 1944. In 1975, a number of the camp staff of that time were put on trial in Düsseldorf but contradictory statements and fading memories made the achievement of a verdict more and more difficult. When judgement was finally delivered in 1981, only one of the accused was given the maximum sentence possible – life imprisonment. Many found the sentences passed on the others lenient to the point of irrelevance.[Transl.]

these lies. This is all part of the present for you in Germany, and the question of National Socialism will remain a contemporary issue for a long while. But what you were saying about forgetting is something I have noticed in myself too – not necessarily in the sense of La Pasionaria's prophetic phrase 'To forget is to betray', but there is so much to do that one sometimes forgets things in the heat of the struggle and relegates them to the past. One doesn't actually forget them, though, – it's just that one gives up thinking about them. But in Germany these are still contemporary issues, and it cannot be otherwise.

II.

E.G.: You have often visited Europe, sometimes for longer periods on health grounds. Have these visits ever taken you to Germany?

H.L-H.: Never to West Germany. But in 1961 I was in East Germany with my husband and visited the former concentration camp of Buchenwald. In 1963 Hans Globke, one those responsible for drafting and interpreting the infamous Nuremberg Laws, who had worked himself up to the rank of *Staatssekretär* [Under-Secretary] in Adenauer's government, was put on trial in East Berlin. Three witnesses were called from Israel to give evidence at his trial, and I was one of them. The trial attracted great attention all over the world. Everybody knew, of course, that Globke, who had played an important part in preparing the ground, politically and legally, for the Nazis' extermination of the Jews, would not turn up to stand trial. But rather than just taking note of the fact with cynical amusement, the authorities attached great significance to it, and in so doing turned the occasion into a political trial which took the whole background into account. Globke was officially summoned to attend. Since he did not appear, the trial was conducted in his absence. It lasted three to four days and was conducted with the utmost thoroughness

The first of the three Israeli witnesses at the trial was a lawyer called Landau, who had been in the Warsaw ghetto and, if I remember correctly, also in Auschwitz. He was deeply moved by the occasion and made an extremely impressive speech. The other witness from Israel, apart from myself, was a young woman, Hava Kökes, from the Yad Hanna kibbutz, who had been in Auschwitz and whose health had been seriously undermined. There were also witnesses from many other countries – Holland, France, Poland, Russia and so on. I spoke in the name of the Jugoslav Jews, and said in my evidence that more than ninety per cent of them had been wiped out. There were formerly 120,000 Jews in Jugoslavia: today fewer than 10,000 were left. I also spoke, of course, on behalf of my own family: eight close relatives of mine had been killed under the most horrible conditions. And I reminded the court that of the six million Jews massacred by the Nazis, over a million had been children – an act of criminal wickedness that has no equal in history.

I spoke too about the Jugoslav professor whom I had mentioned in my diary, who died in Belsen from starvation and disease, as well as from the numerous cruelties to which he was subjected. He was a well-known scholar, an expert in Spanish language and civilisation, in particular that of the Spanish Jews. He had moved in left-wing intellectual circles, many of whose members had been lined up and shot. He had managed to escape to Montenegro but was then deported to Germany with the rest of us.

I arrived in East Berlin some time before it was my turn to give evidence, because I wanted to sit through the whole trial. From the official point of view it was an extremely important event. The papers were full of it. Never in my life had I met so many journalists who questioned me so closely. I knew that this was not just on my account, and I was really impressed. It proved how much significance was attached to the trial, both in the German Democratic Republic and abroad. Israeli papers, especially those of the left, also reported it, so that the Jews In Israel could learn that the Nazi race làws were condemned in the G.D.R. That was very important.

Globke was found guilty, but I cannot remember exactly what sentence was passed on him. In any case, that was incidental. The important thing was the condemnation of Nazi racial legislation, and to this extent the trial served as a kind of postscript to the war crimes trials at Nuremberg. I remember that, although there was no official Israeli representation at the proceedings, the Israeli press said that the trial reflected great credit on the German Democratic Republic. My brother, who is scarcely a left-wing radical, is one of those who were proud that I appeared there as a witness. He saw it as the fulfilment of a kind of obligation to our family. For me personally, I may add, it meant a moral rehabilitation. I am certainly not a person to attach much importance to formal occasions, but this trial has remained an extremely important event in my life ever since.

III

E.G.: Near the beginning of your diary you talk about a serious conflict in your mind before you were arrested, which continued to torment you in the camp. You say it would have been better if you had joined the partisans in the mountains. Why didn't you?

H.L-H.: That was the time when the Italians occupied Montenegro, before the Germans came. Montenegro 'belonged' to Italy until the Fascists surrendered in September 1943. Like everyone else, I was active in the partisan resistance movement against the Fascists. So committed were they to resistance – probably to a greater extent than any other people save the Russians (though the French too had an extensive resistance movement) – that all Jugoslavs could be said to be partisans. It was completely natural and spontaneous, particularly in Montenegro. In Croatia there was a measure of compromise with the Germans, though there was resistance as well. In Bosnia, Serbia and Montenegro, on the other hand, everybody was anti–German. That meant that the Germans had control only of the towns, and even here they were vulnerable, because the roads from one town to another were not safe.

Thus the Germans could only move between the towns in strength and heavily armed, and anywhere away from the road was a source of danger. The Jugoslavs planned everything, well before the enemy surrendered. That may sound rather improbable, but it was obvious to us that the political leaders of the old Jugoslavia would surrender and leave their country in the lurch and that the Generals would turn tail and abandon everything to the enemy. On the other hand it was equally obvious that the people would not surrender, and that the war would go on in the whole of Europe. Of this we were firmly convinced.

Why did I think this way? Because I was with others who all thought the same way. Who were they? They were people who worked in cooperation with the Communist Party. I am not making anything up – we just knew how the situation would develop. Maybe those who were not politically informed didn't understand the position. But I can assure you that the whole Jugoslav people, or at least the great majority, realised that the moment was coming when the people would have to become aware of their power, the moment when control would pass into their hands. When the surrender came, I remember, the soldiers returned to their villages like the remnants of a defeated army. But they took their weapons with them. I saw soldiers trooping back to their families carrying rifles, revolvers and ammunition. It was a matter of course. Those who avoided being taken prisoner returned, not with nothing but with their arms. The women helped to hide the weapons in their cellars. Everyone knew what his job was. It seems hardly possible to believe, but that's the way it was. Everything was spontaneous.

It was, of course, the Party that organised it all, but everyone was so willing to play his part that nobody dreamed that he was acting on orders. Everybody wanted to share in the work. That is why we succeeded, and why there were so many partisans.

I joined the struggle in this way too, and made contact early on with the partisans in Danilovgrad, where I was teaching. Since I was Jewish, I was quickly thrown out of the school, and the headmaster, being an 'efficient' type, also knew that I was in touch with the partisans and therefore wanted to get rid of me as soon as possible. 'Don't be under any misapprehension,' he said to me. 'You're Jewish, and don't forget it.'

The schoolboys, young lads, were very nice to me. In Montenegro every boy of 15 or 16 felt himself to be a man and wanted to become a great hero, taking up arms and joining the fight. And they were right to feel like that, because they really did fight the occupying forces. They were not so concerned with working for their *Abitur* [school-leaving examination] – that took up too much time. They organised a strike, and I helped them. We were good friends, all of us.

Then I received instructions from the partisans to teach the girls in the district first aid. This was during the Italian occupation. Then I joined up with the partisans. There was a great battle near Danilovgrad, in which we were all involved. We found ourselves under heavy fire, and were also attacked by aircraft. We had a great number of wounded and had to see that they were taken to hospital. It was no joke, I can tell you. Dead bodies were lying all around us. Then came the Black Shirts, the Italian Fascist divisions, who were far worse than the Royalists we had been fighting before.

When the Germans came in the autumn of 1943, I was all ready to go up into the mountains. I had stout shoes, an address to go to and all the other things I needed. Then. . . .

There were thirty Jews in Cetinje, only two or three of them young, the remainder elderly people. I arranged with the partisans to take as many of these Jews as possible with me into the mountains, but the sick and old among them felt weak and afraid, and could not make up their minds to come. To fight with the partisans was certainly a hard life. You probably don't realise it, but it wasn't just the danger and the fighting, it was the hard and primitive life itself, the barest possible existence. My husband says that wars today are *guerres de luxe,* in which there are efficient weapons, plenty to eat and all the rest.

This does not mean that I approve of modern warfare – war today has other dangerous and horrible aspects. But you cannot imagine what conditions were like in Jugoslavia at that time. The partisans could not say to people: 'Come and join us in the mountains. You will have a good life up here.' All they could say was: 'If you are going to die anyway, then better to die as free men than in some prison or camp. . .'. We did not know any details but we had heard about how the Germans were exterminating the Jews. But everyone still hoped for the best, and they were afraid of living with the partisans, who could not guarantee that they would have everything they wanted. This was a risk, especially for the sick and the elderly. It was also a political question – the question whether they believed what the partisans said or not.

I was on the point of leaving alone, after much hesitation. Having packed my things, ready to leave the following morning – I lived by myself in a single room in the house of a Montenegrin woman – I was waiting that evening for news of whether the others were coming with me or not.

Three young people came to my room as a kind of delegation, to warn me to consider my decision carefully, for it was common knowledge that as soon as one Jew in any particular group disappeared, the rest were quickly shot. This was the case in Serbia, Croatia and everywhere else occupied by the Nazis. So they asked me: 'Can your conscience bear the thought that in order to go and join the partisans, you will be sacrificing thirty other people? If you go, we shall all be shot.'

I could not bring myself to do it. I stayed with the others and let myself be put in prison. It was scarcely a decision of my own free will – I simply couldn't do anything else.

Maybe I had false hopes, for we speculated that the partisans would know that the thirty of us had been imprisoned, and that since it was already 1944 and we were waiting for the Second Front, they might well be able to finish everything off themselves. . . . And while we were in prison, we did not think we would be deported but rather that the partisans would liberate us. I believed this too, but it was a great illusion. After all, the partisans had never given us such a promise – they couldn't – yet we continued to cherish this hope.

So we waited and waited, until the day came when the Germans said: 'Right, now you're all coming with us.' The Gestapo knew we couldn't expect any help. They took the Jews – only the Jews. The rest, the non-Jews, were left in prison and later liberated. We were taken out and put on to lorries. It was frightful.

Then something happened that was disgusting and at the same time typical. The Nazis lined us up, then each of us had to step forward in turn. They took everything away from us, down to the smallest thing. They had already removed everything from our homes – now, as we were about to be deported, they took away our last possessions of any value. The people were terror-stricken, so brutal and thick-witted were these young Nazis. War is terrible. Young men are taken out and taught to behave like this before they know what life is all about, and then vent their spleen on the weak and the helpless.

'Put everything here – coats, shoes, the lot!' they shouted.

I have weak eyesight and was wearing a pair of dark glasses. 'Give them here!' demanded one of them. I refused. He began to rave and shout, while I tried to explain to him that he did not need my glasses but that I did. 'Who do you think you're talking to, you ugly old witch?' he cried. The others standing behind me were terrified that he might start shooting, and tried to stop me from arguing with him, but I could not help myself. I found it ridiculous to be made to hand everything over. 'I'm not going to!' I cried. He started shouting again, and I saw that I could not get my way, so I just threw the glasses down in front of him. For the moment he was taken aback, but to my surprise he did nothing. I felt a sense of satisfaction. I had not known how he would react, but I was not prepared to give in without a struggle. It made the others glad too, because they saw it was possible to put up some kind of resistance. This all took place in Montenegro, of course, and the partisans were not far away.

I had a friend, a courageous Montenegrin woman, who said she would keep various papers, diplomas and other documents for me while I was away, so that there was something of ours there while we were away. She was very ingenious. Walking right up to the Germans, she said: 'I want to say goodbye to Fräulein Lévy.' I began to hand over the documents to her quite openly. 'What's that?' cried the Nazi soldier. 'They're papers she will need later. I'm going to keep them for her,' replied the woman. 'Do you think you're ever going to come back?' he shouted at me. 'What do you need those things for?' I handed them over to her, then he started to shout again: 'You're never coming back! What are you worrying about your papers for?'

That was the way they behaved, the way they talked.

'You're going to die – that's all there is to it!' they said. So with the words 'Do you think you're ever going to come back?' in my ears, I was transported to Belsen along with the others. The journey took between two and three weeks, under conditions that made it obvious that it was no normal life that was awaiting us. We did not know where we were going, but we did know it was a place where death was close at hand. That much was certain.

As the British army was closing in on Belsen, the SS decided that those of us who could still walk should be sent to Poland and liquidated there. This was their plan. 'You are being taken to Theresienstadt,' they told us. I cannot remember how I came to find out, but it has since become known that in Theresienstadt there were gas chambers ready for those expected from Belsen. But there was no more time for that. The Red Army came across us somewhere between Berlin and Dresden and freed us.

IV

E.G.: I read in a book about Belsen that the train taking the prisoners to Theresienstadt had been travelling for some two weeks before the prisoners were freed by the Red Army in Niederlausitz. Can you describe how you were rescued and how you got back to Jugoslavia?

H.L.-H.: We knew that the Balkans had been liberated and that the Russians were closing in on Berlin, and that we were bound to meet up with them somewhere along the way. But although we knew this, we began to doubt it during the journey, because conditions were so terrible. We were hungry, we all had typhoid, and we had given up thinking about living. Conditions were like those I described in the last pages of my diary. We were no longer fully conscious of what was happening – everything was hazy. Sometimes we were allowed to get out of the trucks, and since the Germans themselves did not really know what to expect, the guards did not watch us so closely. We used to scramble down the railway embankment and pick blades of grass, which we boiled and ate. We were at the end of our tether, and our bodies were like skeletons.

We knew that there were sometimes potatoes to be found, because in Germany they store potatoes under mounds of earth in winter. Sometimes we discovered these clamps when we stopped at a station and they made us get out and fetch water. Those of use who still had a little strength left began to dig some up. But then there would be a terrible scene as all the others rushed to grab some for themselves. Then the Germans stormed into the middle of them, trampling over everything with their jack-boots and beating everyone who had found a potato. That was what happened whenever we tried to find something to eat.

And so the journey went on. Many had already died, and we did not know what to do with the bodies. Then someone gave the order – whether a German or somebody else I no longer remember – to throw the corpses out. They were afraid of the dead bodies. We did not know how much longer the journey would last. In all some few hundred of the 2,000 in the trucks died.

We were all extremely weak and barely able to think straight. A young girl and I found the strength to climb out at one of the stops, where we came across some Jugoslav prisoners-of-war who were coming towards us from a nearby village and shouting to us. We had a feeling they already knew that the Russians were not far away and that the German forces were collapsing. They had been working on the farms in the village and were now making their way to the station shouting: 'Ima li tu jugolovena? Ima li tu jugoslovena? ('Are there any Jugoslavs here?'). It was wonderful to hear, and we shouted back. But they were frightened to look at us. We looked like corpses, while they, having been working on the land, looked fit and well. They came up to us and said: 'Come with us and we'll give you some potatoes!' It was a fairly long way, three or four kilometres, which was a lot for us, but the two of us, the girl and I, went there and collected the potatoes.

Then we started back, but suddenly I found myself alone. I had lost my companion. It was a terrible feeling. Where I got the strength from, I don't know, but I somehow managed to drag a big sack of potatoes back to the train. Then suddenly I saw that the train had gone, which meant that it was still in the hands of the Germans and that they intended to continue the journey with us. I sat down on the ground. It had grown dark, and I did not know what to do.

I went back to the village. There I met the same woman who had given us the potatoes, but I was afraid of her. The Burgermeister had hoisted the white flag, but the village hadn't yet been liberated. I went into the woman's house. I was afraid of her, and she was afraid of me. She didn't know I was Jewish, but that was not the reason. I didn't look like a human being at all – I was filthy and covered in lice. I didn't trust her, because I didn't know what she was going to do to me – after all, it was a German village. She told me to lie down and go to sleep, but I couldn't, so I went into the cow-stall. I didn't want to sleep in a room that belonged to a

German woman, because I didn't know what might happen
to me. I didn't know what to think – whether I would be
rescued, whether they would kill me in the night or what. I
was frightened, like an animal. But there is nothing particularly unusual about this sort of thing – many Jews could tell
you of similar experiences of how they were rescued, what
they were frightened of, their encounters with people who
were not Jews and so on.

The next day the Russian army arrived, and very early in
the morning, about three or four o'clock, I heard the first
Russian soldier. It was a small village and there were only a
few soldiers there. They used to move in with their rifles,
and if nobody fired at them, they took the whole village.

They marched into the village from two sides and I ran
out to meet them, because I could hear it was Russian they
were talking, not German. But they couldn't know who I
was, and began to shout at me. But I was overjoyed to see
them.

The situation was still uncertain, and we still had to
arrange our transport back to Jugoslavia. The Russians said
they couldn't help us and that we would have to find our
own way home. 'Germania vashaya! Germany is yours!
Take what you want and go home!' they told us. But they
couldn't arrange it for us. They had other things to do. This
was before the 8th of May, when the Nazis surrendered, and
the Russians were making for Berlin. So they told us:
'You're free! Now help yourselves!' So we made our own
plans.

I reached Dresden. But there is nothing more of particular interest to tell, for what followed was the common fate
of all ex-prisoners from the concentration camps. We
travelled together down the main trunk roads, whatever

direction we had to go. All manner of people met up with each other – Russians, Poles, Jugoslavs and all the rest. It was like a huge migration. Weeks went by like this, until finally I reached Bratislava.

At this point I'd like to tell you about another incident.

On our journey home we sometimes had to stay a while in some village or other – with the local people, perhaps, or in an empty house. I cannot remember exactly whether it was this side of Dresden or beyond, but in one place I stayed in a house with a German woman, who gave me a very nice room. She was extremely kind, a farmer's wife, and she let me live very comfortably there. By this time I was beginning to look something like a human being again. It was still before the Nazis surrendered. The reason I tell you about this is that I have such a pleasant memory of the episode.

There is something else I remember. The Russians were already in the village. At the side of the house a path ran alongside the railway line, leading to a factory. On the 8th of May, in the morning, I went out of the house, almost as though life were normal. Somebody had said it was all over. Suddenly I saw a young man riding out of the factory on his bicycle. He rode round and round shouting: 'We've won! We've won!' He was a German. It was so good to see, so good for me to hear. When I had passed the factory a few times before, I had noticed that the Germans were listless and just stared. But this man shouted: 'We've won!' Not 'We give in!' or 'The war's over!', but 'We've won!' It was a delight to hear.

E.G.: How did the Germans you met react when you raised the question of the crimes committed by the Nazis?

H.L-H.: I have heard, not once but many times, that people said they knew nothing about such things. Maybe they were afraid or did not want to talk. I can tell you something about this from my experience in Dresden. I went every day to the Soviet commandantura there to ask when there would be a train to take us to Jugoslavia. They couldn't do anything to help us, but I got something to eat there every day, though I was living and sleeping with a German family. The wife of the family was shocked when she heard about these things, and said to me more than once: 'We didn't know anything. They kept it all from us and lied to us. We didn't know they did such things to the Jews.' She showed me photographs of her daughter in uniform; her son was at the front. Her husband had been too old for the army and had gone on working in the factory. He said to me: 'I am glad the Soviet commandantura is here, but they don't give us any food. It's terrible that they don't give us any food'. 'We're hungry – it's disgraceful!' he cried.

I just stared at him. I thought, shall I tell him that I had been far hungrier? Or what shall I tell him? He just couldn't imagine anybody being hungry. He didn't believe what I told him, and his wife kept saying 'We didn't know anything about it.' But he was hungry, so he shouted out. For all that he was an old Social Democrat, and he said to me: 'Let's sing the 'Internationale' together.' So we did. His young son, aged about twelve, was there too. After we had finished, he said: 'Now I'm not frightened of him any more.' This man was around fifty. I doubt if he had been a Nazi. But he was highly indignant that nobody gave him any food. He just didn't understand why. But he did understand that he could now sing the 'Internationale'. That was the second surprise I had.

Another story occurs to me. We arrived one day at some town or village near Dresden – I'm afraid I've forgotten its name – and the place was full of Russian troops. It lay on their route to Berlin, I imagine. There were also a lot of German refugees on the road. The Germans had started to flee as well, some eastwards, some westwards, for they all knew something was going to happen, though they didn't know what. In this way they came across the people who had come out of the concentration camps.

In this place full of Russian soldiers there was a hospital where the sick and wounded could get medical treatment. Here I saw a beautiful young woman, a woman with the beauty of a fairy-tale heroine. She had bandages round both wrists. I was only looking for somewhere to lie down; I did not know where to go and I was terribly hungry. The Russians told us to wait there and they would get us something to eat. This woman waited for a while there too. Then I went up to her and asked: 'What have you done? Why are you wearing these bandages?' She must have noticed that I wasn't German, but that was all, and without asking me any questions, she began to tell me her story: 'I am an officer's wife. My husband died in the war. My father was a doctor. He was a Nazi. I am German, and I cannot bear the thought of a Russian occupation. So full of grief and worry was my father that he threw himself out of a window.'

She went on to tell me that with her husband and her father both dead she could not go on living in Russian-occupied territory and had tried to commit suicide by slashing her wrists. Someone had saved her and taken her to the hospital. Now she was feeling better. I thought that what she meant was that she did not believe that the war could end this way, and for a few moments I wondered whether she was going to ask me something. But in the same instant I felt that we belonged to two different worlds, since she obviously hadn't understood what had happened and thought in the way many people still think today. I could not face the thought of talking to her. I simply realised there was nothing I could say. There was an unbridgeable gulf between us. I just looked at her, and all I saw was that she was a very beautiful woman – nothing else.

E.G.: How long did it take you to get back to Jugoslavia?

H.L.-H.: From the time when we met up with the Jugoslav prisoners-of-war, in the middle of April 1945, until the end of July, when we arrived in Bratislava. As far as Dresden we went the whole way on foot. I came to know Germany well. Sometimes we got a lift for part of the way. In Dresden we found a train, and stole it. 'Steal a train,' people told us. 'It's the only possibility', so we did so, the lot of us – Jugoslavs, Bulgarians, Greeks, Italians and the rest. At the station in Dresden people said to us: 'Get hold of a truck somehow, then find a locomotive that's going in the direction of the border.' And that's what we did.

But it had taken us a long while to reach Dresden – almost two months. We worked out that we had walked about 80 kilometres – not without a break but with stops in various villages. In places where we felt comfortable, we stayed longer and stocked up with food. On the journey I came across a small party of Italian deportees, Communists, who had been in a labour camp, and I travelled quite a way with them. They were good folk – real workers, men of the people, firm and determined. They could get hold of everything they wanted. But they were afraid because they didn't

understand German or Russian, so they asked me to translate for them, because I could speak Italian. So I became
their interpreter. That made them happy, and they got hold
of food and everything else we needed. They were
extremely practical, and we cooperated splendidly with
each other. I was like a queen: they gave me all I wanted, the
best of everything, the best room and so on. They were
good, honest comrades, and I feel a real affection when I
think of them. I travelled with them until we found trains to
take us in our different directions – them to Italy, us back to
the Balkans.

V

E.G.: In connection with your remarks about the Jugoslav
professor I should like to ask a question about one particular
entry in your diary. You wonder about the whole Jewish
question, about what will happen to the Jews after the war,
whether they will go back to their own countries, or
whether they may have become strangers there. You imply
that you are emancipated and assimilated – what Isaac
Deutscher called a 'non-Jewish Jew'.

H.L-H.: So horrified and shattered was I by what went on
in the camp that I began to wonder whether perhaps there
really was a 'Jewish question': perhaps I ought to think
about the matter, which I had never done before. I started to
wonder whether my country would want to have me back,
and whether, if we did get back to Jugoslavia, we would
find that the people there had been influenced by all these
barbarities and become anti-Semitic themselves, even

though the idea had never crossed their minds before. I began to feel frightened, though I had always felt so happy in Jugoslavia. But fortunately my fears proved groundless. In the camp my thoughts were in a state of utter confusion, and you mustn't forget that in such conditions I no longer knew what was true and what was not, or what life was, or what was normal and what was abnormal.

E.G.: Was there any anti-Semitism in Jugoslavia?

H.L-H.: Not really, neither before the war nor after. There were a few isolated occasions, but quite insignificant. It has never been a problem in Jugoslavia, and never will be – certainly not today, when there are at the most only a few thousand Jews in the whole of the country.

When I say there was no anti-Semitism in Jugoslavia, I must explain a little further. Before the Second World War there was a pro-Nazi government in Belgrade. The King and his Cabinet were on friendly terms with the Nazis, and the Nazis, who were like a Fifth Column, behaved as though they were masters of the country. I knew at that time that official anti-Semitic measures were being planned, such as a restriction on the enrolment of Jewish students at universities. I had my university degree and had already become a teacher, but as a Jew, I could never find a good job. This was shortly before the war, 1938–39. I graduated in 1936 and had to wait until 1938 before getting a job at all – merely because I was Jewish, for there were plenty of vacancies for teachers. On top of this, I was made to accept a post at a school a long way from where I lived; there I worked until 1941, the beginning of the war in Jugoslavia.

One could therefore say that there was an atmosphere of

Fascism and anti-Semitism in Jugoslavia shortly before the outbreak of the war, but it did not come from the people, nor was it spontaneous; it emanated from the top. I was made to feel this very clearly by the headmaster of the school in Montenegro where I was teaching after the war had started and the Italians occupied the country. And once somebody said to me in the street: 'Why don't you go to Palestine? There's no place for you here.' But this just struck me as ludicrous. None of my friends or acquaintances behaved in this way – only a handful of rogues. True, one did occasionally hear remarks like this after the occupation had been on for a couple of years, but only here and there. One might ask why, if 100,000 Jugoslav Jews were murdered, the Jugoslav people did nothing to help them, as we know happened in Holland. The atmosphere in Jugoslavia was quite different. Everyone felt it was his duty to fight the Nazis, and the Jews were not given any special treatment. Not only since it has been a socialist country but right from the beginning the attitude in Jugoslavia has been that Jugoslav Jews are Jugoslavs. Every politically conscious Jew was convinced that his real place was by the side of his fellow-fighters. They felt themselves part of the Jugoslav people, as I did. I told you about my connection with the partisans. I took it as a matter of course that my own problems would be resolved in the common struggle. But as I said earlier, the presence of the other Jews prevented me from carrying my plan through.

There is something else I must just say at this point. A moment ago I mentioned Holland. To be fair, I must add a word to what I wrote in my diary about the Dutch Jews and the way they celebrated their Queen's birthday, for I wouldn't be happy to leave it as it stands. The bitterness of

my remarks about the Dutch Jews stemmed from the fact
that we Balkan Jews were subjected to far greater humiliation than they. As a result we developed a kind of inverted
racialism, directed against the 'Northerners.' Today, of
course, when I know so much more, I see it all differently,
and I feel a real affection for the Dutch.

E.G.: Did the situation of the Balkan Jews vary according
to their nationality? Did it make a difference, for example,
whether they were Serbs or Croats?

H.L-H.: Yes, there were differences. The majority of the
Jews from the Balkans were Sephardic – Bulgarians,
Greeks, Serbs. Only the Croats were predominantly Ashkenazi. My brother had the bright idea of uniting the
Sephardim and the Ashkenazim in Sarajevo and forming a
kind of brotherhood. It proved very difficult, but he was
not entirely unsuccessful. We ourselves were a typical family of impoverished middle-class Jews in Sarajevo, where I
was born.

E.G.: So it was rather unusual that you became a teacher.

H.L-H.: Yes, it was, but I was determined to have a proper
profession. That was not so difficult, even in earlier times,
and a person who wanted to learn, and who made the effort,
could get somewhere. Since we were not a wealthy family, I
didn't have to pay school fees. All that was fairly straightforward.

Things were worse for the Jews in Croatia, because the
Croats had latent anti-Semitic tendencies. But I never lived
in Croatia, so I cannot really give you any reliable informa-

tion about conditions there. I do know that Zionism was stronger there: because of the undercurrent of anti-Jewish feeling Zionism was able to establish itself more firmly in Croatia than in Serbia. Hardly any of the left-wing Serbians I knew were Zionists, but some of the Croats were, like my other brother, who was a lawyer in Zagreb. He did not reach the concentration camp but was murdered on the way there, together with a hundred or so other Jugoslav Jews . . .

There were also concentration camps in Jugoslavia run by the Ustaśi – Nazi collaborators, Croatian Fascists – who were violently anti-Semitic and set up extermination camps in Croatia. In one of these I lost a sister and her whole family, and also my brother. My mother and another sister of mine were taken to Auschwitz, in Poland, and murdered there. I learnt about this later. I could tell you many other details but I don't feel I have the strength.

E.G.: Did you give any thought to the 'Jewish question' at that time, or concern yourself with Zionist attitudes?

H.L-H.: My two brothers were Zionists, but I didn't take their views seriously. My elder brother, who is still alive, was an active Zionist and regarded Zionism as something very important in his life. We respected this, and he did not interfere in our affairs. Before the war I moved only in Communist circles in Jugoslavia, though the Party was illegal. I joined all the Communist groups I could find – youth organisations, women's organisations and so on – and when there was work to be done, I joined in. And as a student, of course, I took part in demonstrations. But the thought of Zionism was the last thing to enter my head. I used to discuss it with my brother Michael before the war, but we knew that it was a sensitive subject, and he was well aware that it didn't really attract me. And when I was in the concentration camp, I did not have Zionist questions in my mind but only human questions, the physical question of survival, of what was going to happen to us Jews. That's when I began to reflect on the whole matter.

VI

E.G.: How did you find the situation when you returned to Jugoslavia? Did your experience of Nazism influence your decision to go to Palestine?

H.L-H.: I was very happy to be back in Jugoslavia, and I never dreamt of leaving it. A number of Jews didn't return to Jugoslavia but went straight to Palestine. I was not a Zoinist, and the whole question seemed, so unreal so remote. I just couldn't grasp it. I was pleased to be back in Belgrade – my mother had been living there for the last few years and I went to look for the house where we used to live. This was the new Jugoslavia, and the house had been appropriated – or whatever the word is – by the state. But it was explained to me that I would get everything back, and that I should make a list of things that belonged to me. This I did. It was a purely formal procedure, and a month later all my possessions were officially returned to me. All my possessions – that is, the little house where my mother had lived, some way from the centre of the town.

After my return it seemed quite natural that I should earn my living by becoming a teacher again, and I envisaged no practical or economic difficulties. All I knew was that I was returning to a country where I no longer had anyone save a sister, who was married to a non-Jew in Sarajevo, and the brother I have already mentioned. A second sister had emigrated to the United States. The problem was, how I would feel after all the misery I had experienced? That had created a completely new situation for me. But otherwise it was easy.

Then I was offered a very important and responsible job with Radio Belgrade. They knew that I had a good command of French, and they offered me a post, with political responsibility, in charge of French-language broadcasts. So from September 1945 until the end of 1948 I had two jobs – one with Radio Belgrade, the other in the Information Office of Tito's government, where I was responsible for all publications in French, publications dealing with life in Jugoslavia, the economic situation, the constitution, legislation, culture and the whole development of the new Jugoslav state.

This was a new field of activity for me, one in which I was expected to make my future career. But then I found myself plunged into a complex crisis which put a great emotional strain on me. In my own private life I was living in a void. Perpetually haunted by the memory of my murdered family, I felt as though I were living in a cemetery, or in the middle of a desert. Then came the conflict in me provoked by such tormenting questions as: Who really am I? Am I a Jew? Do I belong somewhere else and not here at all? No one influenced me or tried to persuade me. Then, as I was wrestling with these problems, came the foundation of the state of Israel in 1948. It was an event that echoed round the world. As early as November 1947 Andrei Gromyko, the Soviet delegate, delivered a speech at the United Nations which most people still consider today to have been a Zionist speech. He made a statement to the effect that the Jewish people were entitled to a homeland, for they had been made martyrs, and the conscience of mankind would not be satisfied until they received their due.

At the time this sounded to me quite natural, and it never entered my head to call it Zionist, or to think that the Zionists were right. I was not prepared to entertain such thoughts. And when I eventually did reach Israel, they said to me: 'You people were always opposed to Zionism. Can you see now that we were right?' That's the way they spoke to us. 'Why have you come here,' they asked me, 'if you are not a Zionist? As a Communist you were always opposed to Zionism. Now you can see that it is only in a Zionist state that you can possibly live.' Discussions like this when I first arrived in Israel were agonising. In the Party as well.

E.G.: Were you a member of the Communist League in Jugoslavia?

H.L-H.: After the war I was exclusively in the company of Communists, because that enabled me to spend all my time in close contact with the state apparatus, the administrative centres of power. There were a few Jewish members in the Party, anti-Zionists, with whom I had my first discussions about these matters. When the state of Israel was founded, they declared quite openly that it was an instrument of the imperialists, and that they refused to serve the interests of imperialism. When I asked them what they thought about Gromyko's speech and the fact that he had clearly given his go-ahead to the state of Israel, they replied that that was the policy of the Soviet Union and no responsibility of theirs.

I found myself in a terrible dilemma. There were only a few Jews left, and my Jewish comrades said they were not Jews but Communists – Serbs who happened to have been brought up in the Judaic tradition. They were atheists, they said, and regarded the Jewish aspect as irrelevant. And these good friends of mine, all of whom held important positions, constantly urged me to stay. I could have risen to a senior position in my sphere, but I was not particularly attracted by the prospect, and it was not what mattered most.

This was not the only problem that worried me. There was also the quarrel between Tito and Stalin, which caused something in me to break. The atmosphere was one of hysteria, and I was so confused that I no longer knew who was right and who was wrong. I hadn't yet joined the Party. I wanted to, and I thought I would have made a good Party member. I had been in a concentration camp and had taken up an important job in the new Jugoslavia, and the Party could obviously trust me. But the matter was not so easy. The Communists were not a mass party. I had only been a few weeks with the partisans before being deported. And to the Jugoslavs one wasn't a great hero just because one had been in a concentration camp. Prisoners–of–war and inmates of concentration camps were not treated with any special deference, any more than they were in Russia. They admitted that we had suffered but they pointed out that we had not fought the Nazis, as they had. Today, of course, attitudes have changed, but at that time this was one of their criteria.

The Party also knew that I had shared in the partisans' struggle, and that I had proven my courage and bravery, as they put it; they knew too that I had been an active radical in the old Jugoslavia. But the fact that I had been in a concentration camp, like all the other Jews, made little impression, and when I was encouraged to apply to join the Party, I had to start the laborious task of proving my suitability. It cost me a lot of hard work, day and night, for the first two years in the new Jugoslavia were like a continuation of the parti- sans' struggle. There was an immense amount of work to do, and no one had much time for himself. I took all this very seriously – but I was alone. And after the foundation of the state of Israel in 1948 I began to have misgivings.

As I said, I had applied two years earlier to join the Communist Party. But with the quarrel between Tito and Stalin and at the same time the Israel affair, it was I who refused to join the Party, because whatever questions I asked, I got no answers. All they said was, we can't talk about such things – they are confidential and not meant for the general public. Although I had translated all these documents myself and was responsible for their publica- tion, there were things I was not allowed to know. This made me doubt my position in Jugoslavia still more, and I began to wonder whether my role might not now lie rather in helping to build socialism in Israel.

After I had decided to leave, I realised that there were a lot of good people, important people, who did not want to let me go. I told them all that Gromyko's speech had had a great influence on my decision.

This reminds me of one thing I mustn't forget. It gives me great pleasure to remember these Jugoslav Commun- ists. They were all highly interesting people, with very different mentalities – Slovenes, Croats, Macedonians, Montenegrins, Serbs, all different and all with their own temperaments. And as partisans they all fought together like brothers. This may sound like a romantic fairy-tale but it is true, and Tito was able to fuse these heterogeneous elements into a single unit. To be sure, the political and ideological struggle still goes on, and the situation looks different today, but I am very glad that I was so closely involved in the struggle at that time.

VII

After a ten-day voyage I arrived in Israel on December 31, 1948. My first move was naturally to contact the Communist Party, and immediately after my arrival, while I was living in the immigration camp, I got in touch with them. For two or three months we lived in hut settlements near Haifa, and the Party sent me material to be translated from German or French into Serbo-Croat for people wanting to join the Party. The first text I translated was the very first statement from the United Party – the Declaration on the Union of the Jews and the Arabs, signed by Mikunis and Toufiq Toubi. This was my first political activity in Israel. Shortly after Israel was founded the Arab and Jewish wings of the Party, which had earlier split, were united. The Arab Communists declared this to be the proper and necessary course, and that the united party should be an international Israeli Communist Party which would cooperate with the other (illegal) Communist parties in the Middle East and fight side by side with them. These were fine ideas and fine words. But I remember very clearly that the Arab Communists said that they also found themselves in a serious dilemma, because they didn't know to which side they belonged. 'The Arabs tell us we are traitors,' some of them said, 'and the Jews tell us we don't understand their position properly.' This was the great problem facing the Arabs in Israel (in Jordan they had the Jordanian Communist Party). So the Palestinian Communists in Israel decided to join us in the fight, and from 1948 to 1965 the Party was an international Arab-Jewish party. I still believe today that that was the right course.

When I left the settlement and went to Tel Aviv and Jerusalem, I was already known there, because I had joined the Party. I had very little to live on, and when I started to look for a job, it quickly became clear that, as a Communist, I was not likely to get one. I had a profession and the papers to prove it but everywhere I was turned down, on a variety of grounds, including my membership of the Party. Already at this stage Sephardic Jews were discriminated against. When I told my brother about this, however, he became very annoyed and said it was all a figment of my imagination. But it was very largely true. To be a Jewish Communist from the Balkans and Sephardic as well, was something they were not prepared to accept.

I should add that my husband, whom I met in Israel at this time and who is an Ashkenazi Jew, takes the same view of this matter as my brother. He sees discrimination against Sephardic Jews merely as an insignificant detail in the universal class-struggle. We very often discuss this and other important subjects, but always on the basis of the common class-struggle.

This was the way my Communist 'career' in Israel began. My political work was the only thing that preserved my equilibrium. By calling it a 'career' I am being ironical, for it is not in my nature to be ambitious – but that's a different matter, and part of the problem of being a woman.

E.G.: But wasn't it difficult to move from the world of the Jugoslav Communist Party to that of the Israeli Communist Party, which was aligned with Moscow?

H.L-H.: It happened like this. When I joined the Israeli Communist Party – and I recall this very clearly – Mikunis suspected me of being a Titoist. They themselves were all pro–Soviet. It made life pretty hard for me. Only one of us – he holds a senior post today – was a Titoist. I told them that I held no particular view on the matter and had not been a member of the Party in Jugoslavia. I really did take a neutral attitude. I have since studied the whole subject in detail and came to the conclusion that the policy adopted by Tito was definitely the right one, as history has since shown. They knew in the Party, of course, that I had been politically active in Jugoslavia, but that was no disadvantage, because they realised that it had been my job, and that in this respect I could be of use to the Israeli Communist Party as well. So shortly afterwards I was given the task of preparing the French edition of the Party newspaper.

During the first five or six years the Party had to produce not only the two daily papers in Hebrew and Arabic but also a weekly paper in every language of importance in Israel – Yiddish, French, Hungarian, Polish, Bulgarian and Rumanian. The one small Party published all these papers. At the beginning no one received any money. I was a great idealist, and this made no difference to me. We didn't ask what we were to live on or what we were to eat – we just plunged into the work.

I was fully taken up with my work. Every day I had to read a mass of newspapers, ours and others, and summarise them and also write new articles for French readers, especially North Africans, as well as for the French-speaking Jewish emigrés who did not yet understand Hebrew – I didn't myself to start with, but I swotted it up because I had to be able to translate it. I had first begun to learn it in the 'Beit-Olim', the immigration camp.

Unfortunately I have never managed to learn Arabic. I made a start on it, but that sort of thing has to come naturally, and to me it didn't. It may be a psychological difficulty. And the Arabs in the Party didn't give us much encouragement to do so, because they all spoke excellent Hebrew. When we were together, as, for example, on courses organised by the Party in Nazareth, we were easily able to converse with each other in Arabic or Hebrew as we liked. But as a result they didn't cause us any linguistic problems, so we didn't need to make much effort.

In 1964–65 violent political arguments split the Party and led to the creation of two Communist Parties in Israel – the RAKAH, i.e. the 'New Communist List', and the MAKI, the 'Communist Party of Israel' – which existed side by side for several years. I joined the MAKI, led by Mikunis and Sneh, but only for a short while, until 1968, one year after the Six-Day War. It would take too long to describe all the arguments that went on in the MAKI, which split again at the Party congress in 1968 and decided in 1975 to disband. But I want to say something about the decisive split that took place in 1965, partly because I find the arguments behind it to be still relevant today.

At the time I felt the division was a fairly natural one. We considered the conflicting viewpoints to be irreconcilable. Our Arab comrades made it clear to us that they regarded our line of thought as both harmful and wrong, because we criticised the leaders of the Arab states; their view was, everything the Arabs did was right, and that the blame always lay with Israel. This was too rigid an attitude for us, and not in the true spirit of internationalism. It incensed me, because it was my view that the refusal by all the Middle Eastern states to recognise Israel was a matter that should concern our Arab comrades in Israel as well. Instead they launched into all kinds of accusations. I said to them then what I have been saying ever since, and what I said when I met a number of nice young Palestinian Communists in Paris: 'Tell your comrades that I, Hanna Lévy-Hass, stand solidly behind you. But you are not internationally-minded enough, and don't make enough effort to be so.' On the other hand they are right when they say that we in Israel, even those on the Left, do not sufficiently appreciate why, and to what extent, the Israeli Arabs do not feel at their ease.

At the end of the 1960s the group called SIAH ('New Israeli Left') was founded, with which I was in contact. Then came a period in which my health virtually prevented me from playing any active role, after which I devoted myself to the feminist movement. I was in touch with many people on the Left, irrespective of their party, for my main aim was that they should understand the nature of the women's liberation movement; my own efforts – my own struggle, if one can call it that – were thus always linked with members of the left-wing opposition, most of whom were not in the Party. To a large extent, however, the feminist movement was irrelevant to the great political issues facing Israel.

At the beginning of the 1970s a group of kibbutz members, various left-wingers, members of the MAPAM (United Workers' Party), former Communists from the MAKI, socialists, Zionists, anti-Zionists – a motley collection – founded the MOKED. MOKED means 'focus', and was intended to signify the centre from which progressive ideas radiated. But I am of the opinion that SIAH and MATZPEN ('compass', the name – it is also the name of their paper – by which the Israeli Socialist Organisation is known) and various other left-wing groups have also done good work, especially in the day-to-day struggle and in the class struggle – though it might be more accurate to say that they had positive ideas than that they have actually achieved many positive results.

As you see, there are a lot of things going on, and there is a sense of activity. But there is no common front, and that is why the Left cannot get far in Israel. There are perpetual squabbles and no sense of community, where just such a sense is urgently needed on the Left in view of the dangerous situation in the country. Left-wing circles in Europe tend to overdo the dangers of the Middle East situation, and you are inclined to do the same, I think, when you say that Palestine has become the biggest ghetto in the history of the Jewish people. Certainly, we ourselves talk about a ghetto here, but with a bitter, sardonic twist. Do you know how the Jews here react to the Zionists who come from the Soviet Union? There have been several thousand so far, and many of them have spent time in prison for their Zionist attitudes and activities – hence their name 'Assirei Zion', the 'prisoners of Zion.' In Israel we say that *we* are now the real 'Assirei Zion', prisoners in the land of Zion. It is no liberation for the Jews to come to Israel – the vast majority of American Jews, for example, would never come here. Israel is a problem and a great source of worry for Jews abroad – not vice versa. Jews in other countries are generally in a far better position than those in Israel.

But then, every country is in danger today – one need only think of the possibility of nuclear war, quite apart from the numerous other stage-managed crises, the economic and financial chaos of the West, the fact that a third of the world is languishing in hunger and misery, the growth of terrorism and violence, and all the other dangers and catastrophes that beset the present-day world.

VIII

E.G.: Earlier in this interview you drew attention to the importance of the feminist movement. I found a number of remarks in your diary about differences in the way the men and the women behaved in Belsen. These remarks struck me as being not only the product of your empirical observation of such differences in the concentration camp situation but also as tending to suggest a basic difference in the way the women behaved, compared with the men. You wrote that in certain conditions the women showed themselves to have more strength and stamina, and not to give in so quickly. On the question Food *and* Democracy, which you write about – a question that at first sight looks absurd – was it for you a hopeful sign that it was the women who showed more readiness to sacrifice, or who made the greater effort to embark on concerted action?

H.L-H.: Yes. I also pointed out that it is an objective fact that a man's body reacts differently to hunger and cold from a woman's. There is no question of personal blame. In my view, the male body is not constructed in such a way, biologically speaking, that it can endure as much as the female body. It is a fact – and many doctors say the same today – that a woman can adapt herself better to suffering than a man (not to physical effort, because a man is physically stronger). A man's body suffers much more when subjected to hunger, fatigue or cold. I emphasised this in my diary. As I say, I don't consider it a matter of individual blame, but it is something I observed. I even wrote rather contemptuously about the behaviour of the men. Then I began to wonder – you've probably noticed that my arguments are very contradictory: it's as though I were made for conflicting situations – anyway, I began to wonder whether, perhaps, this was true not of all men but only of a certain class, pampered men who had always been used to a comfortable life. I was certain that the partisans and other fighters were not so weak and didn't behave like that, so my view was not an absolute one. But I can't deny that I did write rather scornfully about them – and not by accident, because the men's behaviour certainly didn't endear them to us.

E.G.: In our conversation in Tel Aviv you made a general remark about your personal life to the effect that for you the present is bound up with all that you have experienced in the past. You said that you could not separate what was happening today from what had already become history, and that the problems you experienced in your thoughts and actions were dominated by this relationship – that is, that what you have thought and experienced in the past is part and parcel of everything you think and do in the present. How does your commitment to the women's liberation movement fit into your development?

H.L-H.: I can't really say that what I wrote in my diary marks the beginning of my intellectual concern with the women's liberation movement. But this only goes to show that even if a woman is not active in the feminist movement, or has no thought of feminism in her mind at all, she still has a feminist outlook in some strange way. I did not make these remarks because feminist thoughts were running through my mind, but when a woman reflects on things, the thoughts she has, are, I believe, always feminist thoughts. It is something quite natural and logical for us women.

As to why I hold feminist views today, that is a much longer story and goes back far earlier than those remarks in my diary. I made those remarks at the time and have nothing to add to them. I have not used them as the basis for any new theory – I just found it necessary to record them.

Feminism is for me a very important question, and we have not devoted sufficient attention to it in our conversation so far. So we must make up for that now. I don't want to bring up the whole range of problems connected with the women's movement – that would lead too far away from our present context. But since feminism is an organic part of my pattern of thought, I should like to make a few basic observations on the subject.

The position of women is a question which is going to become increasingly important in our civilisation as the world develops. It was not always so in the past, but it has become a vital issue in our present age. Everything is changing, and man wants to change everything – whether for better or for worse we can leave aside at the moment. Man seeks to overturn everything, to revolutionise everything in a search for new political, economic and social values. We seek to make everything better and more humane. We explore the planets, we look for new sources of energy – yet where the question of women is concerned, the majority of people think that nothing can be changed and that everything can be left as it is.

That is ridiculous. How can things stay the same in a dynamic world that continually throws up new relationships? A woman cannot continue to be seen more or less as a mere biological phenomenon, a kind of semi-person designed to be a servant, with no influence in society, no claims to a position of leadership, and no say in the way society develops. Why should it be regarded as natural for her not to be involved? Has it been pre-ordained?

These questions are going to become more and more important. There are still countries in the lowest stage of development, where woman is a slave, to be treated as one likes, a person of no account. But there are also so-called highly developed countries in which men have not grasped that it is bad for them as well if women do not take part in everything. The loss to society as a whole is enormous, and men must come to understand this. When they do, they will realise that the emancipation of women is at the same time their own emancipation. Men have acquired far too much power, have control of too many things. They have not always been conscious of this, but society is organised in such a way that men are always the rulers, always make the plans, always carry the responsibility.

What good purpose does this serve? Of course, there are always one or two women there as well. And more women become lawyers and engineers today – in the Soviet Union, for instance. Theoretically everything is open to women in the Soviet Union, yet there are none in positions of power.

How many women are there in the Supreme Soviet? Or in the government of the German Democratic Republic? In other words, this is still a problem in socialist countries today. At the same time, not all women are aware of the necessity for change – many are anti-feminist. It is our task to convince them.

It is a process, moreover, that will take longer in some countries than in others and it will remain on the agenda for a long while yet. But things will continue to develop, and it is the responsibility of women themselves, as well as of others, to see that this development is a positive direction.

Feminism is for me one aspect of the universal class struggle on the part of all progressive people towards a new, humane society, and is an integral part of this struggle. I cannot conceive of a women's liberation movement outside the context of progressive, socialist ideas. I therefore follow the development of feminism extremely closely, to see whether any ideas or activities emerge that might contradict my other principles. The feminist movement must take such forms as will enable it to share in the class struggle and become an inalienable part of it. Simone de Beauvoir has demonstrated that feminism is a progressive struggle in the history of society, and is not separate from the class struggle but runs parallel to it. You can't have one without the other. They are two paths towards the same goal. Thus men are as committed to the feminist movement as they are to the class struggle, and the women in the feminist movement must be equally committed to the class struggle. I fought many a battle for the workers when I was an active member of the Communist Party, but when it came to achieving some-thing for the women, we always found ourselves alone. The men in the Party approved, of course, and laid down guidelines, but it was left to us to carry things out.

At the same time we women naturally went to demonstrations and supported strikes organised by the men, though this had nothing specifically to do with the feminist movement. Why does one talk about the class struggle when a negro, or a Sephardic Jew or an Arab demands equal pay and equal rights, but not when women make the same demands? The class struggle just cannot continue without the feminist movement.

There are, of course, many other aspects of the women's liberation movement and its ideology – social, historical and political aspects, physiological, sexual, emotional, philosophical and cultural questions, and many more – which we cannot go into here.

E.G.: Could you give us a brief description of the development of the women's movement in Israel? In the elections for the Knesset in May 1977, I remember, the feminists put up their own list of candidates.

H.L-H.: Our list was called NASHIM, i.e. 'Women's List'. We had a considerable number of candidates, headed by Shoshanna Ellinger, a very intelligent woman from Jerusalem. Her family has lived in Israel for five or six generations. It was very important for us to have a candidate whose roots were firmly established in the country and who was familiar not only with the problems of the Jewish women but also, to some extent, with those of the Arab women. The feminist movement in Israel started around 1970 and has been growing ever since. A few years later, 1974–5, a militant phase began, with demonstrations, street fighting, clashes with the police, arrests, trials and so on. The movement also produced a number of publications, but they could not, of course, publish all our standard texts in Hebrew. There was a very good anthology of selected texts in translation, and one of the members of the movement wrote a highly informative book on the history of feminism as a worldwide movement, which also examined the position of women in Israel, together with the specifically Jewish aspects and religious problems of the movement. I was active in this work from the beginning and helped to found the Israeli Feminist Movement, the 'Tnua ha'feministit ha'israelit.' Splits later developed in the movement, as they did everywhere else, but in spite of all the difficulties, the work still goes on.

E.G.: I imagine that the position of women in Israel differs fundamentally from that of women in other capitalist countries.

H.L-H.: Yes, it does – and it is a myth that a woman in Israel has equal rights. In the U.S.A. this myth survived for a long while, especially in the minds of American women's rights leaders and Jewish American women. People believed that the position of women in Israel was ideal, and cited the army and the kibbutz. But it is simply not true, and we have succeeded in exploding the myth.

What we have not yet succeeded in doing is to clarify the feminist attitude towards war. On the one hand one hears the view that this is a matter for the men to work out and does not concern women. This view is put forward not on traditional grounds but on the basis that since our history, women's history, has not yet begun, we should not meddle in the politics made by men: we naturally support the state of Israel, because we live here, and we are in favour of peace and security, but how war should or should not be waged, with what means, against whom and so on – these matters are not our business.

This is the one argument. The other, which is supported by the majority in the women's movement, claims that we should join the army on equal terms with the men. One of the basic principles here is that we shall never be regarded as equal to the men unless we carry arms like them. This means that we must have the right to kill and be killed; we must also be eligible to become officers and work alongside men in senior positions in the military hierarchy, since Israeli society is organised on military lines. No man can work his way up or get to the top without the army, and it is the army that determines the course of each individual's career in society.

In this respect feminism seems to amount simply to competition with men, here within the framework of the Israeli political system. A few years ago one of the issues of our newspaper 'Nilahem' (a Hebrew acronym for 'Women for a New Society'; it also means 'We shall fight') contained a discussion on the October war of 1973. In it the question was asked, why women did not take part in that war, and why the war had been lost; further, why women had not been allowed to bear their share of the responsibility for those events, for they had felt humiliated and inferior. This, it was maintained, had been the great mistake in the October war, and the whole paper went on in the same vein. I was both horrified and dumbfounded. I had been a member of the women's movement the whole time and had always regarded our paper as our most vital weapon. Moreover I had always had great confidence in its editors – they must know what they're doing, I thought. I then wrote an article myself on the subject, but it was never printed because the paper folded shortly afterwards. I later distributed copies of the essay but without any success.

In my article I took issue in great detail with these dangerous ideas. How can we say, I argued, that it was a bad thing not to have taken part in that war? Our questioning should start much further back. We should ask, for instance, what good could those policies be that were drawn up without our participation? And if the feminist movement claims that 'our' history has not yet begun, why should we play any part in a men's war? Before we, the women, ask to be allowed to take part in a war, we must insist that a level of understanding and moral responsibility be first achieved in public life as a whole, which will make it possible for women to join men in arriving at a common decision and in embarking on a common plan of action. Why didn't they ask why women took no part in peace movements? If one demands to be allowed to take part on equal terms in fighting a war, why not also in seeking to achieve peace? The women's liberation movement, by its very nature, is a peace movement. A number of women have told me that I am just deceiving myself, and that these are just idealistic illusions that have nothing to do with feminism. This made me realise that their feminism is not mine, and that the movement has many different trends within it which I must observe and analyse. In Israel it has developed in response to the actual situation in the country and the policies that have been pursued there. The majority in the movement are for the government and its policies, and socialists have no influence. That was true, at least, until the spring of 1977 – since then I have spent a lot of time in Europe, for reasons of health.

E.G.: Is there a left-wing feminist organisation in Israel?

H.L-H.: Yes, there was an active group of socialist women
in the feminist movement. For six months we met regularly
every week and studied very profitably together – one
particular work was Engels' *The Origin of the Family, Private
Property and the State*. It is really very surprising that this
work, especially the chapters on the family and the subjuga-
tion of women, is never seriously studied in Communist
circle and study-groups – indeed, it is hardly read at all.

We also discussed in depth other theoretical works, from
France, the U.S.A., England and South America. And then
– an historical event in its way, though a very minor one –
we made our official appearance as an independent group
on May 1, 1975. I succeeded in persuading the group to have
the courage to take part in the May Day demonstration as an
independent feminist unit, clearly distinquishable as such.
Things went on in this manner for some six months, then
came a break, for more or less technical reasons. But I have
been told that the group has re-formed and become bigger.

As to the subsequent development of the feminist
movement in Israel, we put up Shoshanna Ellinger as our
leading candidate. We had a strongly feminist programme
and political platform, and were comparatively objective in
general political matters, which made us acceptable to Arab
women too. I gave my support to our list but we did not
manage to gain a seat in the Knesset. We polled between
5,000 and 6,000 votes but 18,000 were necessary for a seat. If
you look at the case of Flatto Sharon, you can see that
everything becomes possible if you are a man.*

*Flatto Sharon was charged with fraud in France, escaped to Israel and became an
Israeli citizen by invoking the so-called 'Law of Return'. By laying out great sums
of money, and with the help of a powerful propaganda machine, he then got
himself elected to the Knesset so as to obtain parliamentary immunity and avoid
being extradited to France, which had issued a warrant for his arrest and enlisted
the help of Interpol in tracking him down. (Note by Eike Geisel)

IX

E.G.: Isaac Deutscher has written in one of his essays that
Hitler made 'the most significant contribution to the re-
establishment of a Jewish identity', and that Auschwitz was
'the ghastly cradle of a newly-discovered Jewish consciousness.' Is this also your experience?

H.L-H.: I don't think I was lacking in a sense of Jewish
consciousness before Auschwitz. Far from it. But it was
only in the camp that I really felt it strongly. The Jewish
deportees had no one behind them. There was no sense in
which I could resist in the camp. All I could do was to try to
remain human. The Russians, for example, especially in the
concentration camps where rebellions broke out, had
someone behind them; so did the partisans in occupied
countries. But we didn't. This isn't just an empty phrase – it
really was so. It has nothing to do with patriotism. All I
want to emphasise is that it was a terribly difficult situation
for the Jews. Only when they fought alongside the partisans
did they feel safe and content, and in such circumstances
they were able to achieve something.

E.G.: Couldn't the Jugoslav resistance against the Nazis
provide this support? When you wrote about Jugoslavia,
you wrote like a true patriot, and you talk in the same spirit.

H.L-H.: Certainly that was the way I felt. Am I not entitled
to feel and talk like that? But it is an extremely complicated
matter. When I was still in Jugoslavia, I had the partisans to
support me, and felt much happier and could still have
hopes of freedom. But in Belsen I felt as though I had been
left hanging in the air. We had lost all hope and all sense of

contact with the outside world that could have raised our spirits. There was absolutely nothing left. I can understand Isaac Deutscher's reference to a 'new Jewish identity', for it really was new. I had never dreamt of taking up residence in Palestine.

But I must also add that I have always been a highly conscious Jew, even before the war, though not a religious Jew, let alone a Zionist. I have never concealed or denied this fact, even in the most dangerous of situations. It was, and is, a matter of principle, a question of honour. Think of Ilja Ehrenburg's famous words: 'As long as there is a single anti-Semite left in the world, so long shall I go on repeating that I am a Jew.' But before the war I was already an emancipated Jew, assimilated into a non-Jewish environment where there was no anti-Semitism. At the same time it was quite natural that I should remain Jewish and be part of a Jewish reality. In official contexts as well as in my private life I always referred to myself as Jewish. This contradiction is hard for many people to understand, I know. But to me – and not only to me – it poses no problems, and that's the way it was. I have always lived my life in this way, and it reflects the fundamental dialectic of the Jewish character. In one sense you might call me, in the present-day situation, a 'non-Jewish Jew' – though I don't find Deutscher's phrase particularly well-chosen. I would rather call myself a 'universal Jew', if that didn't sound so bombastic – for I don't belong in the company of those really universal Jews whom Deutscher takes as his examples, like Heine, Spinoza, Marx, Rosa Luxemburg, Trotzky and Freud. Perhaps I should rather describe myself as a Jew who is neither prosperous nor chauvinistic but whose heart and mind are open to the whole world, the whole of mankind – for I have a clearly-

defined outlook on the world which is profoundly internationalist.

But why should that make me call myself a 'non-Jewish
Jew?' Other races and peoples – French, British, German,
Dutch, Italian, Russian, Polish, American and so on – have
no reservations about calling themselves by their nationality, even though they may have firm internationalist convictions. For practical purposes, in my everyday life, I have
probably acquired Deutscher's 'new Jewish identity', since I
have lived in Israel for thirty years. I travel to Europe as
often as I can in the interests of my health to try and remedy
to some extent the damage done to my health by my
deportation to Belsen, because I find it difficult to stand the
climate in Israel. But I always go back there, since Israel is
the only home I have. Like other average citizens of that
country, I should like to live there and stay there, but only in
peace, in a normal, friendly relationship with our Arab
neighbours, in a humane and just society. I think Isaac
Deutscher put the question of a Jewish identity in a nutshell,
when he said: 'Only if their search for an identity helps
Jewish intellectuals to fight for a better future for the whole
of mankind, do I regard their search as justified.' For me this
means that all men will find their true identity in their fight
'for a better future for the whole of mankind.'

X

E.G.: You wrote in your diary that the only thing that
mattered was the hope that an entirely new world would
emerge after these terrible war-crimes. But since Auschwitz
and Belsen people only seem to have shrugged off this hope

with scorn. It looks as though the facts about the Nazi concentration camps have only served to help the world at large get used to the idea of mass extermination.

H.L-H.: In a very forthright speech, with the political content of which everybody certainly did not agree, Gideon Hausner, chief prosecutor in the Eichmann trial, said: 'It is not just a matter of the slaughter of the six million who are no longer with us. Even more tragic is that those who are left are sick. It is a sickness that has infected the whole of mankind, a trauma that has inflicted deep wounds on the soul of man.'

With the liberation in 1945 many who had lived through all this were saved, but neither they nor their families are normal people any more. Neither their physical nor their mental health is intact, and if you ask me what effect it has had on their lives, I can only say that it has left scars which grow deeper and deeper as time goes on. Those I know suffer more and more and their ailments get worse and worse. One cannot say that the majority regained their strength and their power to work. They all made an effort to recover and lead a more or less normal life, but no one succeeded, I can assure you.

I would go even further. It may sound a rash thing to say, but I believe that it is not only the survivors who have suffered and are now struggling to find their way in life, but that the whole of mankind seems to have been stricken with a fever. It was a macabre, gruesome period, these four or five years under Hitler, in which terrible things happened which we no longer want to talk about. It has infected the whole world, at least in the west, and many others are carrying the disease around with them. This applies not only to those whose families are directly affected by these experiences but to the whole of society, in my view. And the really tragic thing is that the struggles and problems of modern life have become so complicated that we do not know where this all comes from, what has caused it and so on. We cannot think back to this time or remember all the details. Sometimes a terrible fear comes over me that maybe things are worse now than they were then and that we cannot say that the worst is behind us – perhaps things will get still worse. So my worries about what lies in the future are greater than my concern with what we have suffered in the past.

To come back to the question of what effect the experiences of those years have had on those alive today – it isn't possible to say that one man lives one kind of life and another a different kind. There are not many survivors. Life is hard for all of them – their health has been affected and their ability to work is impaired. They do not feel at ease. What I mean doesn't actually show in their appearance but I know that inwardly they are not happy. For myself, I cannot remember that I have ever felt happy enough since the end of the war to want to sing – in social gatherings, perhaps, but not for myself, alone. I would not say that I am cheerful by nature. True, I joke a good deal – a kind of bitter humour, perhaps – because that's the way I look on life. But I'm not cheerful. Nor am I happy – because there is so much evil left. There is more evil left than good – more in quantity and greater in influence – and this makes me very sceptical. But I still have faith in mankind – a firm faith. It is a faith mingled with all the despair and suffering I have been through, but I still cling to it, in spite of the fact that there is so much to do and to make up for – things like understanding the nature of the relationship between men and women in society as it is and as it should be.

Here I should like to mention something that is very firmly rooted in my mind, something that may perhaps sound a trifle naive. It is a kind of profound faith – 'idea' might be a better word – that has given me a vision – a vision of a more humane future for mankind. Even if I see present-day society as a tragic consequence of the Nazi period – and there are many things today that reflect and echo that period, for it is these past years, the years between 1940 and 1945, that have given modern society its atmosphere of tragedy and impending disaster – I still believe in the progress of society, and in the potential goodness of human nature. I think it is possible to imagine a new future. And although we are aware of what is happening today and may happen in the future, I still believe that the forces for good are strong enough to set the world on a humane course. Naturally I can't know that for certain, but I like to think it is so. If I didn't think this way, I couldn't tolerate the things that are going on today, things I find it impossible to agree with.

I am afraid I cannot claim to be able to do much myself, since my opportunities are very restricted. Hardly being able to do more than think of one's health and the practical things of everyday life is not what I call really living – it is merely existing. Yet I am aware of my past, aware that I tried to achieve something, aware that I refused to give in and that I preserved my dignity. But where present-day events are concerned, I feel completely powerless.

Take what is happening in Lebanon and what led up to it.* I didn't think that this interview would be possible, because I am so preoccupied with the thought of this terrible war, these shameful happenings. Let me just remind you of a passage in my diary, where I wrote to the effect that people who were relaxed, well fed and well dressed just glanced at us for a moment then turned away again. This is the vision that haunts me. One country after another will be overrun, there will be more refugee problems, more arguments over territorial possessions, and so it will go on. Oh yes, there will be international action, and the United Nations will send a peace-keeping force, but that is no solution. A political solution must be found, for there can be no such thing as a military solution – each fresh attempt at a military solution only creates new problems and complicates the situation still further.

But I don't want to give a survey of the present-day political situation or a lecture on politics. You know the situation for yourself. I just meant that there was a time when I was afraid I would not have the possibility or the strength to talk to you about other things. But now we have succeeded in doing so. And it is a good thing that we have, for genuine communication between people, an honest exchange of views on matters of concern to mankind, is in itself a good thing.

Tel Aviv and Geneva 1978

---

* In March 1978 a Palestinian raiding party seized two Israeli buses carrying some forty or fifty passengers, whom they intended to use as hostages for the release of political prisoners. On the northern outskirts of Tel Aviv the buses were intercepted and stormed by Israeli police and army units. Almost forty Israelis were killed in the shooting, among them a large number of children, together with all but one of the Palestinian raiders. The Israeli government gave this incident as their excuse for invading and occupying southern Lebanon. In the summer of 1978 the Israeli army was forced to withdraw under international pressure. As well as continuing to give massive support to right-wing forces in Lebanon, the Israeli army has on more than one occasion intervened directly in the fighting.

THE MASSACRE OF THE EUROPEAN JEWS

Estimated Figures

	Minimum	Maximum	Estimate of the Anglo-American Commission, April 1946
Germany (1937 frontiers)	160,000	180,000	195,000
Austria	58,000	60,000	53,000
Czechoslovakia (1937 frontiers)	233,000	243,000	255,000
Denmark	(less than 100)		1,500 (largely refugees in Sweden)
France	60,000	65,000	140,000
Belgium	25,000	28,000	57,000
Holland	104,000	104,000	120,000
Luxembourg	3,000	3,000	3,000
Norway	700	700	1,000
Italy	8,500	9,500	20,000
Jugoslavia	55,000	58,000	64,000
Greece	57,000	60,000	64,000
Bulgaria (pre-war frontiers)	–	–	5,000
Romania (pre-war frontiers)	200,000*	220,000*	530,000
Hungary (frontiers before the First Vienna Award, Nov. 1938)	180,000	200,000	200,000
Poland (pre-war frontiers)	2,350,000*	2,600,000*	3,271,000
USSR (pre-war frontiers plus Baltic states)	700,000*	750,000*	1,050,000
			6,029,500
less Displaced persons			308,000
	4,194,200*	4,851,200*	5,721,500

* Reliable figures are not available in these cases. Those given are thus only rough estimates.

(Taken from Mickel, Kampmann and Wiegand, *Politik und Gesellschaft,* Frankfurt 1976)

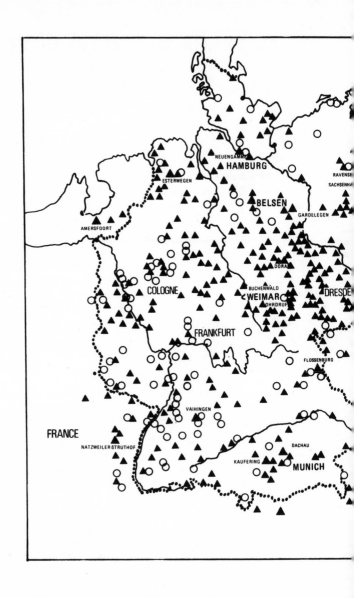

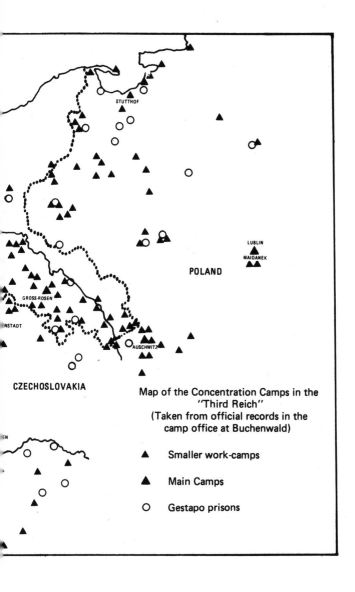

Map of the Concentration Camps in the
"Third Reich"
(Taken from official records in the
camp office at Buchenwald)

▲   Smaller work-camps

▲   Main Camps

O   Gestapo prisons

THE CONCENTRATION CAMP AT BELSEN

Hanna Lévy-Hass was taken to Belsen in the summer of 1944 at a time when the nature of the camp had radically changed from what the SS called a 'preferential camp', like Theresienstadt, to one which was made to take an ever-increasing number of prisoners.

At the beginning of 1943 the foreign section of the SS proposed that Jews holding passports or consular documents from 'enemy countries' should be exchanged for German internees and not be sent to the death camps in the east for the time being. In April the SS gave orders for the establishment of an assembly camp for 10,000 such 'exchange Jews' at Belsen and listed the categories as follows: (1) Jews related to, or with other connections with, influential persons in enemy countries. (2) Jews who could be used as hostages for political or economic purposes. (3) Top Jewish officials. The SS took over for this 'Residence Camp', as they called it, part of a prisoner-of-war camp in which thousands of Russian soldiers had died from starvation, exhaustion, dysentery and typhus in 1941 and 1942. For obvious reasons Belsen never had the status of a civilian internment camp. A bulletin from the economic headquarters of the SS stated: 'We have been informed by the Head of the Security Police that the designation of Belsen as a "Civilian Internment Camp" is for tactical reasons to be replaced by "Residence Camp." This change is necessary because the Geneva Convention requires civilian internment camps to be open to inspection by international committees.' Thus from the beginning Belsen was part of the network of concentration camps administered by the SS.

Between 1943 and the autumn of 1944 some 5,000 Jews, most of them Dutch, were sent to Belsen. They were confined in the 'Star Camp', so called because they had to wear the Star of David on their clothes, and they constituted the largest group alongside Jews from Salonica and Jugoslav, Albanian, North African and French Jews. How little importance the Germans attached to the 'exchange programme' can be seen both from the figure of 10,000 that was originally planned and from the fact that of the Jews taken to Belsen on the pretext that they were to be exchanged, only 357 actually were. It was a process that disturbed the regular timetable of trains carrying prisoners to the gas chambers as little as did economic considerations or what the war situation required. The schedule worked out at a 'timetable conference' in Vienna in May 1944, which provided for the transportation of 12,000 Hungarian Jews to the death camps every day – over 300,000 Hungarian Jews were sent to Auschwitz – was punctiliously adhered to, even though every possible train was needed at this time to take reinforcements to the front. Jewish prisoners in concentration camps were only 'seconded' to industrial firms by the SS within the framework of the so-called 'final solution'. A directive from Himmler dated 9 October 1942 reads: 'I have given instructions that firm measures are to be taken against those who claim to be acting in the interest of armaments production but are in reality only furthering the interests of the Jews.' For those who had allegedly been sent to Belsen as 'exchange prisoners' and had paid heavily for the 'privilege' of not being deported to the 'work camps', i.e. death camps, in the east, the prospect that they might eventually be freed proved a plentiful source of cruel illusions.

From March 1944 the SS also sent prisoners to Belsen who had become so weak from working in armaments factories that they had had to be replaced by others. The first train-load of 1,000, most of them suffering from tuberculosis, arrived from Camp Dora an underground sub-camp of Buchenwald, where they had been employed in atrocious conditions on the manufacture of V-weapons. Ever growing numbers of such 'invalids' were crammed together in a far corner of the 'Exchange Camp' in a so-called 'Imprisonment Camp', designed to accommodate a 'construction party' of 500 prisoners who had been sent to Belsen from various other camps.

The SS pedantically classified the prisoners in their concentration camps and established a kind of hierarchy. In Belsen this classification was carried further in that each category was confined within its own 'sub-camp', which was separated from the others by a high wire fence. There were five such 'sub-camps':

(1) the 'Star Camp', in which Hanna Lévy-Hass was kept and where a terrible system of forced labour was imposed. Even old men were sent out with the 'tree-stump parties' – gangs made to dig up the stumps and roots of trees in the surrounding woods;

(2) the 'Imprisonment Camp', which was run from the start as a 'normal' concentration camp, with convict uniforms, slave labour, *Kapos,* torture and inadequate medical treatment. The number of deaths rose dramatically after the arrival of the above-mentioned train-load from Camp Dora;

(3) the 'Neutrals' Camp', in which several hundred Jews from neutral states (Spain, Portugal, Argentina, Turkey) were interned until March 1945 without being made to

work and under relatively 'tolerable' conditions;

(4) the 'Tent Camp', a compound behind the 'Star Camp', which was occupied from the autumn of 1944 by thousands of women from Auschwitz;

(5) the 'Hungarian Camp', established in July 1944, where conditions were similar to those in the 'Neutrals Camp'. The Hungarian Jews wore civilian clothes with the Star of David (Himmler negotiated through third parties with Jewish organisations for their exchange). In December 1944, after long-drawn-out discussions between the SS and Jewish relief organisations over the *per capita* charge to be paid, 1685 Hungarian Jews were put in a train and taken to Switzerland. Several hundred thousand Hungarian Jews had already been murdered in Auschwitz by this time.

In the 'Star Camp', even under the chaotic conditions that prevailed as the Nazi regime was collapsing, there emerged the features of that 'coercive community' characteristic of the concentration camp system, as described in detail by H.G. Adler for the camp of Theresienstadt and by Hanna Lévy-Hass in her account of Belsen. There was a sophisticated hierarchy among the inmates, ranging from senior prisoner to charge-hand, which served to keep every prisoner continuously enmeshed in a web of terror. As a result a few dozen SS-men in Belsen, who increasingly kept out of sight because of the rampant epidemics and infections, were able to abandon the constantly growing masses of prisoners to certain death from starvation, disease and exhaustion.

As in Theresienstadt, the 'Star Camp' in Belsen housed men, women and entire families, and the illusion that they were receiving preferential treatment played a major part in destroying their psychological balance. Rumours about plans for an alleged exchange in the near future, or about the intentions of the SS in charge of the camp, or about the situation at the front had a great impact. They circulated as reports from an imaginary news agency, the JPA (Jewish Press Agency), a name that became synonymous with rumour.

With the continued advance of the Allied armies in the winter of 1944 the SS transported the surviving prisoners in concentration camps near the front into the interior of Germany. These journeys often lasted for weeks, whether death-marches or transportation in open freight trucks in freezing temperatures and without food. Thousands broken by slave labour were taken to Belsen to 'recover', and masses of prisoners evacuated from Auschwitz and its associated camps, from Ravensbruck, Gross-Rosen, Mauthausen and elsewhere (the majority of them women) also arrived. In consequence the population of Belsen grew rapidly. At the end of November 1944 there were some 15,000 prisoners, at the end of January 1945 approximately 22,000, by the end of February 41,000 and at the moment when the camp was liberated in the middle of April, about 60,000.

With the appointment of Josef Kramer as commandant, an expert in concentration camp affairs who had been adjutant to commandant Höss in Auschwitz and had himself been commandant of the Auschwitz II camp (Birkenau), together with the deliberate overcrowding, the systematic starvation, the widespread epidemics and diseases, and the constant use of torture, the conversion of Belsen into a 'proper' death-camp was complete. A few days before the camp was surrendered to the British troops, the 'exchange Jews' had been taken away in three train-loads. This provided formal evidence that for a number of months the camp had been serving as a marshalling point for the loads of prisoners evacuated from other camps – not that the 'exchange Jews' had been treated any better than the rest of the inmates. The place had become a huge junkyard of human remains which, after the 'corpse-processing plant', the crematorium, had stopped working, were just regarded as so much garbage, and treated as such. And this was what it looked like when the British arrived – a garbage dump of thousands of corpses piled on top of each other, a stinking mass of putrefying bodies.

If one compares Belsen with Auschwitz and the policy of systematic murder in gas chambers, one can see how little there is to choose between mass murder through the efficiency of modern industrial techniques and the traditional methods of human mass destruction. The prisoners in Belsen died from planned starvation and deliberately encouraged epidemics; only comparatively few were shot or died from being tortured by the SS guards. In March 1945 alone over 18,000 died there or were found to be dead when their transport arrived. Before the camp was finally liberated, the number of those who had perished from starvation or disease had risen to 35,000, and even after the liberation, despite the medical aid given by the British, who discovered huge quantities of food and drugs stored in the camp armoury, a further 13,000 died as a result of their sufferings and deprivations.

The Belsen war crimes trial took place before a British military tribunal in Lüneburg between 17 September and 16 November 1945. In the dock were thirty-three members of the SS and eleven *Kapos,* prisoners who had been given certain supervisory duties in the camp. A large number of the SS guards were not affected at all, since the British only put on trial those whom they had found in the camp on their arrival.

The trial was conducted according to the procedures of a British court martial, that is to say, the accused were treated like British soldiers, each of whom had to be found individually guilty. Eleven SS men were condemned to death, eleven more and eight of the *Kapos* were given prison sentences; fourteen were found not guilty.